Online Recruiting

Online Recruiting

Recruiting

How to Use the Internet
to Find Your Best Hires

DONNA GRAHAM

DAVIES-BLACK PUBLISHING
PALO ALTO, CALIFORNIA

This book is dedicated to my father, Samuel Culmo ("Papa"),
who passed away on July 23, 1997. Papa taught me many things before he left this world,
but his death taught me even more. I learned abruptly how precious life is and how in
an instant we or someone we love can be swept from existence without any warning.
Maybe that is why I decided to get started on my lifelong goal of writing a book.

I would also like to thank my loving family—
my husband of eighteen years, Ron, and my sons, Steve and Tommy—
for their love and support during the writing of this book.

Published by Davies-Black Publishing, an imprint of Consulting Psychologists Press, Inc., 3803 East Bayshore Road, Palo Alto, CA 94303; 800-624-1765.

Special discounts on bulk quantities of Davies-Black books are available to corporations, professional associations, and other organizations. For details, contact the Director of Book Sales at Davies-Black Publishing, an imprint of Consulting Psychologists Press, Inc., 3803 East Bayshore Road, Palo Alto, CA 94303; 650-691-9123; fax 650-623-9271.

Visit the Davies-Black Publishing web site at www.daviesblack.com.

04 03 02 01   10 9 8 7 6 5 4 3 2

Library of Congress Cataloging-in-Publication Data
Graham, Donna M. (Donna Marie)
    Online recruiting : how to use the Internet to find your best hires / Donna Graham.
      p. cm.
    Includes bibliographical references and index.
    ISBN 0-89106-142-8
    1. Employees—Recruiting—Electronic information resources. 2. Internet
advertising. I. Title.
HF5549.5.R44 G72 2000
025.06′6583111—dc21   99-089260

FIRST EDITION
First Printing 2000

Contents

PRAISE FOR ONLINE RECRUITING

"A great resource for people looking to learn more about online recruiting. It provides in detail everything you need to know about job hunting using the Internet."

—*Gary Resnikoff, President, Careermag.com*

"Well written and researched. An excellent book full of state-of-the-art tools and strategies to allow any recruiter to join the Internet revolution. A must read if you are going to win the 'war for talent'!"

—*John J. Sullivan, Professor and Head of HR, College of Business, San Francisco State University*

About the Author

Donna Graham is founder and president of Careers R Us, a consulting firm in Rochester, New York, that specializes in innovative recruitment techniques for job search training, testing and skills assessment, career counseling, and outplacement services. While helping job seekers learn to utilize the power of the web in their job search, she became intrigued and began actively researching this technology.

Graham received her bachelor's degree in business and organizational development from Roberts Wesleyan College and her master's degree in career and human resource development from Rochester Institute of Technology. A human resource consultant with more than fifteen years of experience, she serves as a peer reviewer for the U.S. Department of Education on Vocational Rehabilitation in Washington, D.C. Before founding Careers R Us Graham worked in a human resources capacity at General Motors, and she is currently on the faculty at Roberts Wesleyan College where she teaches courses in human resources and organizational management over the Internet and in the traditional classroom.

She is a member of the Society for Human Resource Management, the National Human Resources Association, and the Rochester chapter of the Organization on Internet Recruiting

Introduction

Sometime in the late 1990s there was a great explosion. Scientists around the globe are still collecting data and analyzing what happened—and how it happened so quickly and without any warning. The explosion started in the 1980s but didn't reach noticeable proportions until the final eruption sometime in 1998. It changed the way we conduct business and the way we shop, and it disrupted the recruiting process that has been in existence since the invention of the printing press. This explosion, of course, was created by the Internet. The growth of the Internet has been astronomical—with global estimates at over 200 million users. When you take a quick look at the statistics in this Fast Facts table you will begin to realize the true magnitude of the Internet explosion.

Many of us may be wondering just how much we need to be involved in this Internet explosion. We realize we need to do something, and most major companies have probably tried some form of online recruiting, but has it been successful? How do we measure our success in online recruiting? Are others (maybe our competitors) getting better results and more placements? Is there a better site or service we could use to maximize our results? Are we just playing a game of trial and error, hit or miss—praying our errors and misses will be few? These are just a few of the many questions this book will help you answer. *Online Recruiting* will greatly reduce the guesswork and provide

FAST FACTS

Global Internet Usage Estimates

Africa	1.72 million
Asia/Pacific	33.61 million
Canada & USA	112.4 million
Europe	47.15 million
Latin America	5.29 million
Middle East	0.88 million
World Total	201 million

Source: Data compiled by Nua Internet Surveys, New York, current May 1999.

you with information and proven strategies to help you succeed in hitting your target smack-dab in the middle.

The Internet explosion created an awesome opportunity for the recruiting industry. There are now millions of chances to attract millions of job seekers. The word *networking* has taken on a whole new powerful meaning—it no longer means just keeping in touch with contacts we know personally. *Global* networking is now possible. We have the capability of stretching our fiber-optic fingers across the globe at the speed of light. However, this also entails a tremendous learning curve. Our recruiting process and recruitment tool kits must be updated and continually improved in order to stay current with new technology and new ways of recruiting candidates. This book will help you through the learning process and will provide techniques to keep you up to date on the new technology on this laser-speed information highway.

So how many people are actually using the Internet in the United States? According to *Cyberatlas* ("More People Online . . . , 1999), 83 million adults sixteen years and older are using the Internet in the United States. This number, according to IntelliQuest Research, makes up over 40 percent of the U.S. population. Bill Gates, CEO of Microsoft, Inc., estimates that by the year 2001, more than 60 percent of all U.S. households will have PCs and 85 percent of those homes will have Internet access (Gates, 1999). With all this technology in our homes and offices, there is a cultural transformation going on. Over half of U.S. households use a personal computer, and most of those households are wired to the Internet. This has significantly affected our daily lives and routines. The way we communicate, look for jobs, shop, and receive information is more digital than ever. Lucent Technologies, a successful high-technology company in the communications business, printed the following paragraph on the back of its 1998 annual report: "While you were reading this annual report (about half an hour), 2,800 people logged onto the Internet for the first time, 4,000 new customers signed up for cellular phone service, 19 million voice-mail messages were left, and 154 million e-mails were sent." With 154 million e-mails in a thirty-minute time frame, it's no wonder the U.S. Postal Service keeps raising the cost of postage stamps.

E-mail is one of the most popular features of the Internet and for recruiting online. According to the 1997 American Internet User Survey from Cyberdialogue, 85 percent of adults online use the web and 75 percent use e-mail. This same survey found that 20 million Americans consider the Internet indispensable. Indispensable? These must be the same people who told all their friends about the Internet and caused the one million new users to sign up with America Online (AOL) in the first five weeks of 1999. What did we do before this wonderful invention? We used the U.S. Postal Service more, shopped for cars and antiques in stores rather than online, and searched for jobs in the newspaper or in trade magazines. The point I'm trying to make here is that most of us are still getting our news from the morning paper or television, and we are still shopping at malls and at regular old-fashioned stores. The only difference is that we have a few more choices available to us now that the Internet is here.

The same is true for recruiting. Job seekers are still looking for jobs in the newspaper, but they now have more choices available to help them with their job search. Some of the strategies in this book will show you how to tap into the many ways job seekers have to hear about your job openings. An excellent example is through the medium of e-mail. As the above statistics illustrate, e-mail is a very popular method of communicating, and you will learn about some innovative techniques for using e-mail as an effective recruiting avenue.

With this phenomenal growth rate of online users, no wonder most of us feel we don't have a good grasp of the vast world of online recruiting. With close to 30,000 job boards, such as Monster.com (www.monster.com) and CareerMosaic (www.careermosaic.com) fighting for our attention, what's a recruiter to do? Along with all this screaming, there is also extensive spending going on. Forrester Research projects employer spending on recruiting online will increase from $105 million in 1998 to $1.7 billion in 2003. These estimates are triple the estimates Forrester made in 1997. We need to know why billions of dollars are being directed toward the online industry. What messages are we hearing from the marketing campaigns, and, more important, what messages are the job seekers hearing?

A good example of the type of marketing campaign driving job seekers to place their resumes online is a Monster.com television commercial that had only child actors and went something like this:

> "I want to be downsized when I grow up."
> "I want to be forced into early retirement."
> "I want to be underpaid for what I do."
> "I want to be a brownnoser."

The message was loud and clear, and it was aimed straight at passive job seekers—people who are already employed, often highly skilled, and maybe somewhat discontent in their present jobs. Passive job seekers may just be thinking about changing jobs and not actively searching yet. These are the people most recruiters and headhunters want to attract because they have the skills, experience, and training required for the job they need to fill. These candidates usually are capable of contributing almost immediately. So this means we need to look at not just one area of online recruiting to maximize our efforts, but all three key areas. These key areas are job postings, resume surfing, and recruitment advertising, which will be discussed separately in Chapters 1, 2, and 3, respectively. Job postings and resume surfing are primarily going to reach the serious job seeker, and recruitment advertising is geared toward both the serious job seeker and the passive job seeker.

Chances are the next employee you hire or the next resume you review will be a job seeker currently employed by someone else. You must have something to offer candidates that they don't have with their current employer. When you start thinking about what you can do for the employee rather than what the employee can do for you, you start attracting more qualified candidates than you can handle. I know this is the complete opposite of what has worked in the past and contradicts everything you've been taught, but you will soon find out that to survive in the recruitment arena for the next millennium, you must think and act differently. Acting differently will require action on your part to explore this new territory. You will need to welcome technology with open arms.

Labor Shortage

One major contributor to the success of online recruiting is the fact that we are dealing with scarcity in almost every job classification. IBN:interbiznet.com is a niche-consulting firm located in Mill Valley, California. Each year the company produces an analysis of the online recruiting industry. In its 1999 Electronic Recruiting Index "Executive Summary," this company predicted a modest shortage of 2.3 million workers in the U.S. economy by January 1, 2000. Unemployment rates in the United States are at an all-time low (most states' rates are lower than 4 percent, and the unemployment rate for college graduates nationwide is less than 2 percent). This means that there aren't enough skilled, educated, and capable job seekers to fill all of our available job openings. When unemployment levels are high, employers have very little trouble filling their open jobs. During times of high unemployment, recruitment advertising sites don't have to spend millions of dollars on advertising to target the passive job seeker—as in the case of Monster.com. Personnel departments would be fielding the influx of unsolicited resumes, phone calls, and applications to the point of exhaustion. It makes you sometimes wonder which of the two evils is worse—high or low unemployment?

So most of the job seekers we are dealing with are most likely already employed. That's why some recruiters are having better success than others with online recruiting. If you're not getting the attention of those passive job seekers, you may not be having much luck finding qualified candidates online. You want to be going in the same direction as job seekers, so you need to be paying attention to marketing campaigns on a national and local level to achieve good results with online recruitment. One of the best-kept secrets to online recruiting is to reach this passive audience. Chapter 3, on recruitment advertising, focuses on this topic. This strategy is geared toward the active job seekers as well as the hard-to-reach passive ones.

Survey results from the Electronic Recruiting Index 1998 survey of thousands of recruiters indicated that over 60 percent of respondents had experienced labor shortages in areas other than information technology (IT). However, IT and other highly skilled candidates are extremely scarce. I would guess most companies have a minimum of one IT position open at any given time. Most have more than one opening to fill—in software engineering, hardware, networking, database management, or some other highly skilled, in-demand, computer-related field.

This unfortunate fact of life is the reason this book references a few more high-tech web sites and IT scenarios than other fields. You will also find useful web sites and strategies that work well across all disciplines, whether you are recruiting nurses, doctors, lawyers, computer engineers, office administrators, or any of the hundreds of job classifications in between.

Many experts in this area predict that by 2002 more than 98 percent of all companies will have one or more job postings online. Why does it work so well? I believe the answer is in the numbers. There were millions of workers displaced during 1997 and 1998 and millions more decided to leave on their own to change careers or jobs. Even though unemployment rates are at an all-time low, downsizing, reengineering, and reorganizations in the workforce have been causing some massive redeployment throughout the United States. The job changes may be a result of corporate reorganizations or simply job seekers taking control of their own fate and changing careers. The Internet opens up the latter scenario to greater possibilities by giving job seekers a chance to search out opportunities in other states or countries—and they can do this in their pajamas at two o'clock in the morning. To be successful with online recruiting you need to be creative in your strategies, especially to tap into the passive crowd. An excellent example would be attending a trade show or business show in a particular industry to scout for new talent. You may be thinking, "I've been doing that for years." Good for you. In order to recruit the scarce fields of talent, you need to be hanging out in the online world and the real world with the types of candidates you're looking for.

Advantages of Online Recruiting

As with all of life, it would not be wise if we did not look at both sides of the story, the advantages as well as the disadvantages of online recruiting. The advantages of online recruiting definitely outweigh the disadvantages—otherwise there would be no need for this book. But we must take a cautionary look at the disadvantages and be realistic in our approach to

FAST FACTS

Global Growth on the Information Highway

>> **83 million adults 16 years and older were using the Internet as of April 1999**
Source: *Cyberatlas, IntelliQuest Research*

>> **60%+ of all U.S. households will have PCs by 2001**
85% of those homes with PCs will have Internet access by 2001
Source: *Bill Gates,* Business at the Speed of Thought

>> **98% of all companies will have one or more job postings online by 2002**
Source: *ERB: Electronic Recruiting News 1999*

>> **1 million new users signed up with America Online (AOL) in the first five weeks of 1999**
Source: *ERB: Electronic Recruiting News 1999*

>> **$105 million dollars spent on online recruiting in 1998 will increase to $1.7 billion by 2003**
Source: *Forrester Research*

>> **20 million Americans consider the Internet indispensable**
Source: *1997 American Internet User Survey, from cyberdialogue.com*

>> **60% of recruiters surveyed reported they experienced labor shortages in areas other than information technology**
Source: *1999 Electronic Recruiting Index Executive Summary*

>> **Labor force shortage in America was expected to be 2.3 million workers by January 1, 2000**
Source: *1999 Electronic Recruiting Index Executive Summary*

Notes regarding statistics: There are many surveys and compilations going on this very second to determine the various usage and statistics of the online world. All this fuss is causing an interest in a new way of doing business called e-commerce or electronic commerce. Therefore, many marketers are working hard to gather as much information about the online population as they can. However, this is not an exact science and all kinds of measurements and various parameters are being used. You can look at studies and results from the well-known Forrester Research and get a very different set of online statistics from those compiled by another research firm. The statistics and data vary from survey to survey, expert to expert, not because one is more accurate than the other, but because different surveys use different measurement methodologies. Therefore, I have made every effort to use statistics from various sources in order to count in different methodologies. So just remember when we are talking millions and billions, the statistics may be off a couple of million here and there. For the most part, the numbers are as accurate as they can be in this very dynamic and extremely high-growth environment.

strategic planning in order to increase our success rate. So what are the major contributors to the success of online recruiting? I have ranked the top three advantages as follows:

1. Cost
2. Speed
3. Reach

COST

The number one advantage of online recruiting is cost. All three advantages are important, but in the world of business the bottom line is what really counts. There is minimal risk and you may actually invest more of your time than money into online recruiting. This advantage may have been obvious to you. You probably figured, "Hey, everyone else is doing it, it doesn't cost that much, why not give it a try?" Or you may still be in the exploration stage and may have picked up this book to find out what all the commotion is about. By the time this book is published, there is a very good possibility that just about everyone will be using online recruitment to some degree, given the growth rate of companies coming online to post their jobs. If the predictions prove correct, and close to 98 percent of all companies were indeed recruiting online by the year 2000, the cost should continue to stay low.

As more and more competition enters the market, the costs normally are driven down, but I haven't seen this happening in the online world. The demand for candidates may be keeping the cost the same or higher. However, as long as online web owners do not get too money-hungry, costs should remain affordable to most businesses. Online recruitment involves little overhead and few employees, and requires no printing press or paper, delivery trucks or delivery personnel. But there are other costs involved. Recruitment sites have to pay for servers to store all the resumes and information, and someone has to design the fancy web pages, sell the advertising space, and do all the computer-geek stuff—and, you know, the bottom line is making money. Some recruitment sites are spending millions of dollars on television commercials, airing during Super Bowls and such, in order to create brand awareness and drive people to the site. Somebody is going to have to pay the hefty price of these massive recruitment advertisements, and I bet it won't be the job seekers—it will be the recruiters and employers. Don't worry, some of the best things in life are still free, and I will share some great free or low-cost sites with you in Chapter 5.

A $12,000 print ad in the *Chicago Tribune* may generate twenty or more resumes. The same ad posted online to a job board may result in a similar response rate for a fraction of the cost, depending on where you post the job. Because of the low cost and high circulation of posting online, the major metropolitan newspapers have been losing some of their precious recruitment advertising dollars to online recruitment. Newspapers charge by the column inch or per line, and now they have to compete with Internet job sites where you can post unlimited advertisements and have unlimited space with an unlimited audience. So it took them a while, but most newspapers have jumped on the Internet bandwagon and joined up with Careerpath (careerpath.com). Careerpath is a digital duplication of most major metropolitan newspapers' Sunday classified advertisements loaded onto a web site. What I have found very interesting is that Careerpath actually competes with newspapers' major advertising dollars—from recruitment agencies such as Bernard Hodes, TMP, Nationwide, and others.

Recruitment agencies have developed their own web sites in order to stay competitive, and these have been very successful. Along with newspaper head honchos, recruitment agency heads were shaking in their boots and realized they had better do something quickly. They would say things like, "Oh, you don't want to put anything up on the Internet—you'll get swamped with unqualified candidates and all kinds of weirdos will be knocking on your door." The newspapers and recruitment agencies might have even believed this nonsense, but the Internet fought some of the biggest, meanest, and most powerful recruitment campaigns and won. They won for two simple reasons—it works and it's very cost effective. I'm not saying newspapers don't work—they have been the number one medium for matching candidates with open positions—but times are changing. The Sunday newspaper isn't the only option we have in our recruitment tool box anymore. The low cost of online recruitment caused the masses to rush to the Internet in droves, and the results have kept them coming back for more.

In May 1999 CareerMatrix posted the percentages in Chart 1 (see page 10) online showing a breakdown of recruitment spending. The number of participants and other demographics of this survey were not shown; however, 25 percent is still a hefty piece of the pie and, converted to revenue, represents millions of recruitment dollars taken away from newspapers. Just about every communication medium is starting to target the job seeker and tap into the millions of dollars of recruitment revenue. Even radio is becoming a popular way to push job information and job commercials. (This approach has the ability to target both passive and active job seekers.)

CHART 1	RECRUITMENT SPENDING PERCENTAGES
Description of Recruiting Activity	**Percentage of Revenue Spent on Recruiting**
Newspapers	49%
Outside Recruiters	20%
Online Recruiting	25%
Job Fairs	4%
Other	2%

On the other hand, Internet recruiting, if you're not careful, can build up some pretty hefty costs—both tangible and intangible. To determine potential cost, some questions you need to ask yourself are, Will I need to hire any additional people? Will I need to hire a web master to develop or improve my web page? How will training and maintenance be handled? How will this change the way our human resources department handles recruiting efforts? Will Internet recruiting help reduce my HR staff, or will I need to increase staff? You may feel that you do not have to change any of your current processes, and that your answer to all these questions is *no*. However, there is always a cost when you invest your time or your human resources' valuable time. There is always a hidden cost, and you should plan on allocating a specified amount of time, money, and resources to the online recruiting process.

So a major advantage of online recruiting can also be a major disadvantage. In reality, even if you don't hire personnel and you use just the free sites to start Internet recruiting, you are investing time—and time is money. How much time are you willing to invest? How much time can you afford to invest? Are you going to cut back on your print media advertising budget? Will you have to go to fewer job fairs? If you have a very small recruiting firm, your time will be more costly than if you have a larger firm with more human resources. If you decide to use commercial

CHART 2	COST ADVANTAGES AND DISADVANTAGES
Advantages	**Disadvantages**
Low cost	Consider and budget direct costs
No cost if utilize only free services	Consider indirect costs
May be able to reduce HR staffing levels	Training personnel
Minimal risk or no risk	Hiring personnel
Minimal investment or no investment	Time involved in online recruitment

sites with membership fees, you must ask yourself how much of your advertising budget to allocate to Internet recruiting. These are some of the questions you and your staff will have to evaluate to determine what is best for your individual company. If you decide not to eliminate or cut back on any of your other advertising options, you have just added another operating expense to deduct from your profits. You now have to check e-mails, review resumes (sometimes many more than before), post jobs online, update online job postings when they are closed or filled—and the list goes on and on. You will have to carve some time out of your daily schedule or delegate these tasks to another person in the staffing department. How much are you willing to invest and budget for this? Few things in life are free, and time is our most precious commodity.

SPEED

The second advantage of online recruitment is speed. How many times have you called your recruitment agency on a Wednesday only to find out you missed the deadline for Sunday's employment section? So you're busy doing all your human resources stuff (hiring, firing, training), and before you know it, another week flies by and you miss your deadline again for placing the ad. Now your hiring manager leaves you nasty e-mail messages inquiring why the job hasn't been advertised yet and why he hasn't seen any resumes for his opening. You then panic and call a couple of your recruiter friends, informing them of your opening and asking them to send you some resumes. You spend another couple of days clarifying and updating the requirements of the position with the recruiters. You finally remember to fax the job in time for the Sunday paper deadline and you can relax now. Or can you? Now the recruiters will be sending you a slew of resumes and the newspaper will probably generate a flood of paper resumes and phone calls (even though you put in the advertisement "NO PHONE CALLS PLEASE"). Candidates read those words and say to themselves, "They don't mean me, I'm sure. I'll show them just how eager and interested I am and call them first thing Monday morning!" So how much time has passed by now? Three weeks or more? We will probably never completely discard our standard method of placing newspaper advertisements to find new employees, but I believe as time goes on we will use print media for recruitment less and less. We will use print media instead to drive people to our web addresses and for name recognition.

With the Internet you can get your job posted and ready to be viewed in a matter of seconds, and the possibility of receiving a response from a candidate has shortened to a matter of minutes rather than weeks or months. At the same time, this speed has also allowed your competitors to receive the same job seeker's resume in their in-boxes. You now have to work harder and faster to compete. If you're recruiting high-in-demand candidates, you must act quickly. You have to be ready to coun-teroffer candidates considering two or three job offers simultaneously. What can you offer a candidate that is better than what your competitor down the street or around the globe can offer? If you remember nothing else from this book, remember to "ask yourself not what the candidate can do for you, but what you can do for the candidate." As a career counselor I tell job seekers to ask just the opposite when they are seek-ing positions: "Ask yourself not what the employer can do for you, but what you can do for the employer." That is how a job seeker will land a job and how you will hire a great candidate.

CHART 3	SPEED ADVANTAGES AND DISADVANTAGES	
Advantages	**Disadvantages**	
Job postings reach job seekers almost immediately	Competitors' job postings reach job seekers just as quickly	
Can reduce turnaround time in hiring employees, resulting in positions being filled faster and more efficiently	May need to improve processes to handle paperwork processing, approvals, and so on or risk losing candidates to someone else	

REACH

The third significant benefit of online recruiting is reach. The Internet uncontestably reaches more people than any other medium. Where else can you turn to have your information read by just about anyone, anywhere in the world? Newspaper account executives will tell you their circulation is 10,000 or 180,000, depending on the geographic area, and it sounds impressive until you compare those numbers to the millions of people the World Wide Web reaches. Reach is also the most significant disadvantage of using the Internet for recruitment. You're going to be reading a lot of resumes from people living not only across town, but across oceans and in faraway countries. When we post jobs online, we are posting them for the world to see, and in the process we're opening up Pandora's box. Resumes start coming in from virtually every nook and cranny of the globe.

With global recruiting we must also deal with some other important issues. Some of the barriers to overcome are visas, immigrant status, relocation allowances, language, and cultural barriers. It has been my experience that many companies are having difficulty dealing with these issues, and some do not want to bother with H-1B visa sponsorship due to the expense of legal requirements and the like. Some companies have been forced to consider this avenue because they have a critical need for specialized people and they have exhausted all other methods of recruiting

CHART 4	REACH ADVANTAGES AND DISADVANTAGES
Advantages	**Disadvantages**
Reaches millions of job seekers	Reaches millions of job seekers not in your geographic area or country whom you may not be willing or able to pursue due to visa restraints or limitations
Ability to staff for satellite offices and throughout the United States without setting up personnel in other areas	Increased paperwork and resumes—opens up Pandora's box to receive more resumes (many not qualified or willing to relocate)
More diverse workforce	Cultural barriers need to be overcome
Ability to fill critical staffing needs not able to be met from candidates in the United States	Added expense and legal paperwork required to hire from other countries

in the United States. You might also look north to our Canadian neighbors to find technical talent. Thanks to NAFTA, a Canadian job seeker just has to show up at the border with a few documents (a written U.S. job offer, work experience, and a college degree) in order to work in the United States. If you decide you need to sail the open seas to look for talent, Chapter 1 has a section dedicated to hiring individuals from other countries.

As we move toward a more global economy and more businesses have a presence in other countries, these issues will become less of a problem. Lack of diversity in the workforce will be a problem of the past, and the workplace will be a better place because of the wide variety of talents and abilities coming together. If you are currently working for an international company and dealing with global recruitment, the reach of the Internet is the best news you've heard so far. With online recruitment strategies, filling a job opening in Japan or Australia can be done without sending HR staff and managers to faraway destinations.

So, there you have it—the major advantages and disadvantages of online recruiting. Most companies have already decided that the advantages far outweigh the disadvantages and have been experimenting with online recruiting for some time now. Are you in the less than 5 percent of employers still waiting on the sidelines? I must caution you, staying on the sidelines watching is more risky than joining in and playing the game. If you start small and experiment, you are more likely to have success without feeling like you're drowning in information overload. Take things slowly and you won't feel so overwhelmed. I highly recommend that you take advantage of the low-cost or free sites to test the waters before diving in. My bet is your customers and your competitors are probably already swimming and practicing their strategic dives to win at this. I also know all the statistics and experts agree that online recruitment is growing and will continue to grow until all employers have their jobs or some portion of their employment listings online. Some will continue to post their jobs to recruitment sites, and some may have an online presence driving people to their web site due to their products or services. Those companies may have an icon for visitors to select to inquire more about job opportunities within the company. We are at a point now where even the small mom-and-pop shops in rural areas have a web site. Job seekers expect to find jobs online and have added this to their job search tool kit, where I believe it will stay as long as the Internet is available and continues to provide useful information and services adding some value to our lives.

Summary of Topics

This book is divided into two parts. Part One is "Strategies and Tools of Online Recruiting" and Part Two is "The Best Places on the Internet for Online Recruiting."

PART ONE: STRATEGIES AND TOOLS OF ONLINE RECRUITING

Part One covers the three basic areas of online recruiting—job postings, resume surfing, and recruitment advertising. These areas will be detailed in Chapters 1, 2, and 3, respectively. Chapter 4, "Tools and Tricks That Make It Quick," is full of the hottest strategies to help you stay up to date with online recruiting trends and increase your efficiency and productivity when you are online. Part One is broken down as follows.

Chapter 1: Job Postings

Job postings are your critical job openings, complete with job descriptions, posted on your home page or other Internet recruitment sites. The hardest thing to get used to with online job postings is writing the content. Unfortunately, too many human resource people do not devote enough time and attention to this most critical aspect of online and offline recruiting. Most of us are used to trimming our job notices to the fewest lines possible to cut costs of advertising in print publications. Almost the opposite is the case for posting jobs online. We can say as much as we want to in the online recruiting world. Actually, the more we tell the job seeker about the job, company, culture, and so on, the better off we are. For example, if a job seeker performs an online search using keywords such as "Systems Analyst" and "Unix," she may come up with 200 or more job openings matching these key words. If your job opening doesn't say something to spark her interest, she may just click on by to the next listing that gives a little more detail.

Remember, job seekers don't want to waste time talking to employers or recruiters about jobs they are not interested in any more than you want to talk to a job seeker who doesn't fit your job requirements. So don't be misleading or illusive regarding your job openings. This topic is discussed in detail in Chapter 1, complete with samples and illustrations of powerful job postings that will intrigue even the most job-content employee and attract the high-demand candidates. You will learn about the three most important factors for increasing your response rate when writing a job posting. This chapter also covers some of the legal aspects of recruiting online.

Chapter 2: Resume Surfing

Resume surfing is the second basic part of online recruiting. This is the process of sourcing resumes, searching resumes, and researching ways to increase the number of qualified resumes for your candidate pool. This is usually the most time consuming and frustrating part of online recruiting. Searching for candidates online and offline can make you feel like you are searching for a needle in a haystack. With the millions of resumes online right now, and hundreds being added every minute, you need the fastest possible strategies to find just the candidates you're looking for. For example, in April of 1999, a sales representative from the popular Monster.com informed me that this site was receiving an average of 4,000 resumes per day. Following a prime-time Super Bowl advertising campaign, he said they received an average of 6,000 resumes per day. So you're probably asking yourself right now, "With that many job seekers looking for work and that many resumes online, why can't I find qualified candidates to fill my critical job openings?" It may be that you're just not looking in the right places.

Chapter 2 is devoted to resumes and to helping you search all the online options available to keep your in-box overflowing with qualified resumes. You will be introduced to resume distribution services, great resume databases, and services that provide automatic e-mail notification of resumes matching your requirements as soon as they hit the Internet. So whether you're looking for ways to hunt for resumes online more efficiently or, like me, you prefer the method where resumes come to you, you'll find some services and techniques to make the search a little easier.

Job seekers like the idea of submitting their resume online in the hope that a recruiter or potential employer will search them out and offer them their dream job. Some will do just about anything to get their phone ringing. Some candidates are learning quickly to include key words in their

FAST FACTS

Monster.com Number of Resumes Received

>> **6,000 per day during**
   Super Bowl campaign
>> **4,000 per day on average**

Note: Monster.com spent $26 million on recruitment advertising in 1998

resumes in order to pop up in employer search queries—so beware of the key word abusers. They are skilled in fooling the system rather than skilled in their actual expertise. This is a common problem in recruiting and not limited to the online recruiting world. You also need to know how to find the less obvious candidates hiding on personal web pages or in faraway galaxies on the web. So how do you find these candidates or get them to find you? This question leads to Chapter 3, "Recruitment Advertising."

Chapter 3: Recruitment Advertising

Recruitment advertising, the third basic part of online recruiting, helps the job seeker find you and your web site rather than you finding the job seeker. It is just as difficult for the job seeker to find you as it is for you to find him or her, if not more so. The job seeker has been inundated with thousands of web sites, job sites, hot sites, cool sites, cool commercials, and so on, and he or she is just as confused about online recruiting as you are. So the trick to recruitment advertising is to make it painless and effortless for the job seeker to find your job openings on your recruitment site. Chapter 3 covers some proven strategies used by leading companies to drive candidates to their front web door. These strategies appeal to passive job seekers. Because they are already employed and not fully pledged to job seeking, passive job seekers are probably not included in a resume bank or searching job postings. They are not actively seeking out jobs when they are online. Instead they are looking for information for their job or personal life, shopping for a new car or computer, e-mailing or participating in a chat discussion group. These are the people most recruiters and headhunters want to attract. They have the skills, experience, and training employers are looking for because they are already employed in a job similar to the one they are trying to fill. This is where recruitment advertising takes on a whole new meaning.

Recruitment advertising is probably both the most critical component of online recruiting and the most overlooked. It involves extensive marketing of your web site. The marketing media can be newspapers, trade journals, radio, online, or a combination of several communication channels. The online component of this method is usually a purchased advertisement—banner, button, or flashing icon—to attract job seekers to your home page or job board. Many companies, having invested heavily in their internal web sites, are finding that the number of job seekers visiting their site isn't as high as they had hoped. In the blockbuster movie *Field of Dreams*, the theme was, "If we build it, they will come." This may work in Hollywood, but not with web sites. We need to be putting up road signs, billboards, and flashing icons on as many high-traffic web sites as possible in order to get high numbers of visitors. Even well-known companies such as Microsoft, Inc., use this method to attract passive job seekers to staff over eighty hires per week (Gates, 1999).

I sometimes refer to this strategy as the flycatcher approach. You have heard the saying, "You can catch more flies with honey than with vinegar." As job seekers are visiting other sites, you try to catch them with some sweet honey. Once you get their attention, you need some sticky stuff to keep them at your site. This method offers a job seeker the chance to learn more about the company and career opportunities after following the hyperlink. A hyperlink is a stepping stone to another site—the browser doesn't have to type in the URL address. For example, if XYZ Company wants to attract job seekers to its site, it may purchase a banner advertisement on America Online or another high-traffic job site. When job seekers visit America Online's career center and see XYZ's banner advertisement, they can click on the banner and be quickly zapped over to XYZ's employment home page. Recruitment advertising is the *push* method of recruiting online. The secret here is attracting job seekers to you rather than you trying to find them. This strategy helps you target passive job seekers. This chapter shows you what types of sticky stuff some innovative companies are using to attract job seekers.

Chapter 4: Tools and Tricks That Make It Quick

Chapter 4 covers all the online tools and tricks available to you. These tools and tricks will help you stay current with the latest online recruiting news, trends, technology, software, and useful information. This chapter also shows you the sit-back-and-wait approach to recruiting. Technology has provided us with some very efficient tools to help us recruit candidates almost effortlessly. You will see how to source candidates while you or they are sleeping and from distances far, far away.

PART TWO: BEST PLACES ON THE INTERNET FOR ONLINE RECRUITING
According to Forrester Research, there were 500 job sites online in 1995, 6,500 sites in 1998, and 28,500 in 1999. Job sites seem to be growing at an exponential rate and were predicted to reach over 100,000 sites by the year 2000. That is why Part Two of this book is dedicated to helping you sort through some of this information by providing a directory of the best places on the Internet. Chapter 5 discusses the best of the free or low-cost job posting services. Chapter 6 provides a comparison of the leading web sites for recruiting employees. Chapter 7 discusses recruiting trends for the new millennium.

Chapter 5: The Best of the Freebies
One of the best ways you can maximize your recruiting investment is by using free or low-cost sites. Chapter 5 covers the best places on the Internet that offer free or minimal-cost job posting services and ways to search resumes for free on the web. Leading job sites include Yahoo and America's Job Bank, among others. This chapter can help if you are just starting to explore online recruitment sites. With little risk (only your time is invested) you can begin online recruiting today without any contracts to sign, hassles to deal with, or payment agreements to worry about.

Chapter 6: Comparisons of Leading Web Sites
Chapter 6 compares leading web sites and available Internet resources to help you make the right decisions about finding, recruiting, and hiring employees. You will learn how to stay clear of the scams and discover proven strategies for successful online recruiting. Some people compare the rush to the Internet to the gold rush of the nineteenth century—neither is very regulated, and just about every scam artist knows this. So how do you tell the gold from the gold plated, and how do you avoid pitfalls and costly mistakes? How do you avoid sending checks to businesses you don't know much about? Such information as who's really running the site or who actually owns the job board really makes a difference. I like to know

who I'm doing business with—their partnerships, alliances, and methodology—before making a decision. By looking at web sites from the inside, outside, flip side, backside, and upside, you'll get a better picture of who you are really sending your recruitment dollars to—and this in turn will help you steer clear of costly mistakes and scams.

Chapter 6 also shows you where to find the best cyber hangouts for the particular candidate you are seeking. If you're looking for MBAs, college students, information technology people, or any combination of these, this chapter will point you to their neck of the woods. You will learn about some very good niche sites targeting only the particular industry or field you may be looking for. You will also find out what some of the leading recruitment sites are doing to compete with these niche sites and how you can utilize both to improve your success rate.

Chapter 7: Forecast for the Future of Online Recruiting

One of the most critical aspects of HR management is planning. In order to succeed we need to find and attract the best people available using the most cost-effective methods available. Online recruiting is in a continual state of change and improvement. Chapter 7 reviews the latest and most futuristic possibilities of online recruiting. You will get a quick peek at what is just around the corner as well as what to expect in the distant future. Unfortunately, the labor shortage is going to get worse before it gets better. This chapter will help strategic planners start putting a plan together for the next five to ten years and beyond.

APPENDIXES

There are three useful appendixes at the end of the book. Appendix A is for the reader with no experience on the Internet. Appendix B offers answers to frequently asked questions about online recruiting. Appendix C lists all the web sites and addresses mentioned in this book.

Appendix A: Getting Started

This book is presented in a simple user-friendly format designed to assist anyone involved in recruiting new employees, from beginners to advanced users. You do not have to be a computer guru to dabble in

Internet recruiting. If you have thought about using the Internet as a recruiting tool but weren't sure how or where to begin, Appendix A will help. This section covers the absolute basics—general information and tips and tidbits to help you get started in this fascinating online world.

Appendix B: Frequently Asked Questions About Online Recruiting

For some quick facts, you may want to go to Appendix B. Here you will find responses to some of the most common concerns regarding online recruiting. Some sample questions answered in this section are

"Should I post salary information?"
"Should I post all of my jobs online?"
"How long should I post my jobs online?"

Appendix C: Directory of Web Sites

Various web sites are mentioned throughout this book. For your convenience, Appendix C provides a complete, alphabetized directory of all the sites and web addresses (URLs) mentioned in the book.

GLOSSARY

I have written this book more for beginners and dabblers in online recruiting than for the proficient computer expert. It is in simple, user-friendly language (as opposed to computer-geek language). Actually, I have tried to use as few technical terms as possible. However, from time to time, even more advanced readers may come across an unfamiliar word or two. The Glossary explains the abstract, high-tech language you may come across—if not in this book, then while recruiting online.

REFERENCES

There are very few books written on the topic of online recruiting for the human resource professional or the recruiter. Many references throughout this book were from online surveys and statistics or from books targeted for the job seeker. As I mention several times throughout this book, it is wise to put your job seeker's shoes on and become more aware of what they are being told by such experts at Joyce Lain Kennedy. For further reading, I recommend the books mentioned in the References.

Mission

In writing this book, I set out to provide you with strategies and tools to help you find, recruit, and fill your critical job openings faster and more efficiently by utilizing the power of the web. The intent was not to be all-inclusive, but to give you some insight into the industry's service leaders and to introduce the available options. I have mentioned numerous services, software applications, and companies without intending to make any endorsements; rather, I wanted to give you an opportunity to learn about some of the hottest technologies available to make your job easier. If I have left out some fantastic service, it is probably because I either didn't know about it or didn't feel it had been on the market long enough to establish any credibility. Many services are here today and gone tomorrow, so I tried to limit my discussion to services I've used personally or that have been around for at least a year or two.

I felt the need to write this book because I was so frustrated with the lack of information available (all in one place) to help someone in the recruitment area hook up with candidates and fill job openings. I received my bachelor's degree in human resources management and my master's degree in career and human resource development in 1995. During my years of undergraduate and graduate schooling, I never learned anything about electronic recruiting. I didn't take classes such as Electronic Resume Batching 101 or Introduction to Web Job Postings. I had to learn how to do all these things on my own. I learned the hard way—from hits and misses, mistakes and successes. If you are feeling as inept as I was at first, please be assured that any amateur can become very proficient in a short period of time. This book will give you all the ingredients you need to mix up a great recipe for delicious hiring and recruiting. It's up to you to add or leave out a dash of this or a pinch of that.

Online recruiting is fascinating, exciting, and forever changing. Unfortunately, too many recruiters all over the country are struggling with how to make sense of all the new technology. With thousands of recruiting sites and services to choose from, at some point you may have experienced an information overload. Whatever your history with online recruiting, the goal of this book is to increase your success rate by maximizing your recruiting efforts, reduce your failure rate, and help you utilize the power of online recruiting. This book will show you how to use the latest online strategies and tools currently working for leading companies and recruiters around the globe.

At the end of some chapters I have listed some key concepts, as shown in the following example.

KEY CONCEPTS

>> A passive job seeker is someone who isn't really job seeking at all and more than likely is already employed in a job like the one you are trying to fill.

>> Recruitment advertising helps you reach passive as well as active job seekers.

>> To be successful with online recruiting you need to utilize all three key areas of online recruiting: job postings, resume surfing, and recruitment advertising.

>> The top three advantages of online recruiting are cost, speed, and reach.

>> Ask yourself what you can do for the candidates, not what they can do for you. Only then will you start attracting more qualified candidates.

>> What messages are job seekers hearing from marketing campaigns? Pay attention to national and local marketing campaigns to get good results with online recruitment.

>> In order to recruit from scarce fields of talent, you need to hang out in both the online world and the real world with the types of candidates you're looking for.

>> If you build it, they will not come—unless you attract them with the power of recruitment advertising.

Part One

Strategies and Tools of Online Recruiting

Chapter One

Job Postings

With thousands of jobs posted in one database alone, you are competing with literally millions of others when you write your online job order. That's probably why you get ten different responses when you ask ten different recruiters, "Are you having much success with online recruiting?" Some are and some are not. I believe the main culprit in the failure ratio for some recruiters may be their job descriptions. Writing effective job descriptions and job postings is something that is rarely talked or written about. I'm not sure why this critical component of online recruiting has not been given the attention it deserves. If you find yourself wondering why "nobody is responding to my job posting" or thinking "I paid good money to have it posted on the leading job board and I received only one resume," you might give more thought to how you write your job orders.

As you may recall, the three components of online recruiting are job posting, resume surfing, and recruitment advertising. Job postings will be discussed in this chapter—where to post your job openings will not. There are thousands of choices available, and Part Two will show you where most job postings are landing as well as review the best sites. However, if you're thinking about skipping this chapter because you just want to get to where you should post, you should know that "how to" is much more critical than "where to" in improving your success with online recruiting. In this chapter you will learn the best strategies to increase your exposure so your posting stands out among the millions of other jobs posted, and the best techniques to get job seekers to respond to your posting.

Job postings are descriptions of job openings posted on the web. This chapter focuses on everything you need to know about writing job postings for the online world, time-saving techniques to get your jobs posted efficiently, and three items to include in your job postings to increase your response rate. You will also discover the ten key characteristics of successful job postings, see samples of powerful postings, and get tips to protect your company from costly discrimination lawsuits. Other topics include great places to help you find custom-written job descriptions, benchmark studies, and competitive salary information.

How to Be Outstanding in a Field of Millions

One of the biggest challenges in recruiting online is to make your job posting stand out from the millions of others so it will be seen and read.

FAST FACTS

Web Site Job Postings as of June 1999

America's Job Bank
(www.ajb.dni.us). 958,481

Yahoo Classifieds
(www.yahoo.com). 360,000

Headhunter
(www.headhunter.net). . 290,000

Total 1,608,481

As you can see in this Fast Facts table, the number of jobs posted in 1999 on the three leading sites alone was close to 2 million. That number is even greater today, with more and more companies migrating to the Internet to recruit. When you also take into consideration all the other online companies, your job postings are hanging out with some 150 million other web pages.

So how do you get your jobs to stand out among 150 million other web pages, all screaming for attention? You need to pay special attention to what works and what doesn't work when you post jobs online. There are three strategies to increase the odds of your jobs being seen and responded to.

1. Use the ten key components of effective online job postings.
2. Make recruitment advertising effective.
3. Carefully choose the best job board(s) to meet your needs.

The first strategy, using the ten key components of effective online job postings, requires including all the pertinent information that has been proven to increase your job posting's chances of being seen and responded to. The second and third strategies are also critical to job posting success. Effective recruitment advertising works like a magnet to job seekers and will be detailed separately in Chapter 3. Carefully choosing the best job board(s) is also critical to increasing your chances of being seen online and will be discussed in Chapter 6. Here let's focus on the first strategy.

FAST FACTS

150 million other web pages are competing with your job postings

28,732,786 job postings online in 1998

Source: 1999 Electronic Recruiting Index Executive Summary, produced by Interbiznet, a niche-consulting firm located in Mill Valley, CA. Each year IBN produces a detailed survey and analysis of the electronic recruiting industry.

TEN KEY COMPONENTS OF ONLINE JOB POSTINGS

The following characteristics of an effective job posting have been proven to increase your chances of having your job posting read as well as responded to.

1. Key words/category
2. Job title
3. Salary
4. Company profile
5. Job description
6. Job specifications
7. Education level required
8. Location
9. Benefits
10. Contact information

Although all ten components are important, the top three are the most critical. Why? Because most job sites allow job seekers to narrow their search by entering a category or key word. The key word is listed first in order to ensure that your posting is returned in the search query. Then job seekers will see a list of results according to the key words selected. The results usually return a job title, company name, and salary range. Many sites also allow for a more defined search, such as job specifications. Once you've accomplished being noticed in the search results, you must make sure the job posting intrigues the job seeker to act and respond.

In the online world of recruiting, we have to change the way we think. We used to think small—the shortest possible words, many abbreviations. Why? So we didn't make the newspaper industry any richer and ourselves any poorer than we had to. With online recruiting, we don't have to scrunch, squeeze, or shrink our job postings anymore. Therefore, one of the topics explored in this chapter is how to write a better job description. Making a job description longer and more detailed doesn't make it better, just longer to read. Ask yourself this question every time you write a job posting: "What would it take for me to change jobs?" Most likely, job description, location, salary, benefits, corporate climate, stability, and opportunities for growth are all important items you consider during a career transition. So when you are writing the online job ad, make sure you include as much information about the job and the company as you possibly can. A well-written online job description has enough information to inform but not bore job seekers, and is intriguing enough to get them to act.

1. Key Words/Category

Key words and category are ranked first and are extremely critical to improve your online success. Why? Because specifying the appropriate category helps reduce the millions of job postings to manageable results for the job seeker. If you don't select the appropriate category and the most common key words, there is a very slim chance that your job posting will ever be read. Most online job banks have separate search fields labeled "category," "industry," and other key words to refine the search results for job seekers. This has both positive and negative results. On the one hand, key words provide more specific, customized searches for the job seeker; on the other hand, they can have an adverse impact on both the job seeker and the recruiter. For example, say you want to fill an executive position for director of sales and operations for a manufacturer of electrical engineering components. One of the job specifications is that the candidate must have an electrical engineering background and a college degree in engineering. You can choose only one category from the list below in which to place your job posting. Which one would you choose?

- Management
- Professional and Executive
- Sales and Marketing
- Engineering
- Manufacturing

If you choose the wrong category, a great candidate may never know about your job opening. So which is the right category? This is tricky because many jobs cross over into professional, management, computer, and other categories. If you aren't able to choose several categories, you need to make sure you choose the one where the majority of your target job seekers would search. So the answer is really that all of the categories are appropriate possibilities. If at all possible, try to select sites that allow for more than one option. HeadHunter, for example, allows recruiters and job seekers to choose up to five categories. You may have the world's best-written job description, but no one will ever read it if it doesn't pop up in the search results.

Many job banks also allow job seekers to refine their searches by identifying key words. You should include them in your job title if at all possible. For example, imagine all the possible categories under which job seekers might look for AS400 programming positions: as/400, AS400, as 400, programmer, programming, programmer/analyst, programmer / analyst, analyst, programming manager, and management. If you really need an AS400 programmer, you should make sure AS400 is in the title. Technology is continually improving—most sites have sophisticated soft-ware that takes into consideration the many variations of job titles (such as AS400 programmer), but others do not. So just make sure you know whether the site you're posting to is capable of interpreting variations of case-sensitive words and common abbreviations of job titles. If not, you may not get the results you are hoping for and may need to monitor the key words, changing them as necessary. If the site you're using doesn't have a separate field or area in which to type in key words, you should include a separate paragraph in your job posting, titled "key words," to list all the key words applicable to the job. That way, if a job seeker is searching key words, your job posting will turn up in the search results even if the title isn't something he or she typed in.

One more important item to remember—the terms *manager* and *management* are also very popular with job seekers. Many candidates are seeking hands-on managerial jobs or project management jobs where they can use their computer expertise. If your position involves some management responsibilities, you should include the word *management* in the key words to increase your responses.

2. Job Title

The job title is another area that tends to get completely overlooked when job postings are placed online. Do you realize how frustrating it must be for a job seeker to log onto a job board and find hundreds of jobs with the exact same title? Let's take the job title "manager" as a working example. Manager of what? If a job seeker types in the word *manager* on any popular job board, I'm positive he or she will have hundreds of job matches. What are the chances this job seeker will stumble across your management position? There is a very good chance your position will only be read by someone who is desperate, unemployed, and bored, who has lots of time. Even in this scenario, the odds are small that your job ad will be remembered. Don't make this mistake. You need to inform the job seeker what or who he or she will be managing. To get noticed online, you should be industry specific, yet as general as possible. Rather than simply using a "manager" title, use specific industry areas such as these:

- Sales Manager
- Office Manager
- Retail Manager
- Training Manager
- Human Resource Manager
- Customer Service Manager
- Healthcare Manager
- Financial Services Manager
- Information Technology Manager

By using industry categories such as IT, healthcare, retail, and so on in your managerial job title, you enable the job seeker to easily choose the appropriate titles of interest. However, you don't want to run the risk of screening out candidates who are qualified but don't think they are because they are not familiar with the job title. An example of being too specific would be a title such as "Patient rep-administrative associate of ambulatory services." Many job seekers would assume this is very job specific, requiring specialized job skills they might not have. In reality, this job could be filled by anyone possessing a GED or a high school diploma. So if you're specific—but not too specific—you'll have better results and more responses to your job postings. Also, if room is available, add words such as "Hiring Bonus Paid" or "Awesome Career Opportunity" after your job title to attract more job seekers and stand out in the crowd.

3. Salary

Whether to post salary has been a subject of debate in the human resource field for a long time. The debate is still going on with regard to print media. My audits have shown that including a pay rate or range leads to a higher rate of response—sometimes three times the rate of response for similar jobs without salary information. There are different reasons HR professionals decide to leave salary off the job postings. Sometimes it's because of company policy or because the compensation package isn't competitive with those of other companies in the area. If you feel your company's salary offer is lower than the benchmark or that by listing salary you won't have room for negotiation, you are fooling yourself. Do you really want to talk to seven people about a job they're not interested in once they realize the pay is too low? I would rather have two candidates respond who are willing to accept the salary range of the position than twenty job seekers with higher pay expectations. In my opinion, always put in a salary range—even if the range is quite wide. This still leaves you with opportunity to negotiate with candidates depending on their experience, education, and other qualifications.

If you're not sure whether your salaries are competitive for your industry or geographic area, you can find additional information and receive online help with comprehensive salary data and surveys. Here's a simple little web site you may find interesting: Wageweb. You can review general data on benchmark salaries for more than 150 positions for free. The positions are broken down into easy-to-navigate categories: HR, administrative, finance, information management, engineering, healthcare, sales/marketing, and manufacturing. For a membership fee of $100, among other benefits you can view all the general data and sort them by geographic area and size. The goal is to provide HR professionals with compensation information to help them keep their most important asset—their people. You can find Wageweb at www.wageweb.com.

Another cool site to check out, especially if you handle quite a few relocations per year, is Homefair. The site is located at www2.homefair.com/calc/salcalc.html. Sponsored by realtors, it is geared to assist job seekers contemplating relocating. Here candidates can key in their current city, state, and salary, as well as their destination city and state. The salary calculator compares costs of living and informs job seekers of the salary they would need to make in the new city to afford a comparable lifestyle. For example, if one were making $100,000 in Rochester, New York, he or she would have to make $141,000 if relocating to Fremont, California. This site also has crime reports and other helpful community facts for the serious job seeker considering moving.

America's Job Bank, sponsored by Uncle Sam, is also an excellent place to find market information, marketing trends, employment outlook, career information, and numerous statistics on the labor force. You can find wages, trends, and salary information on just about any job at this site too. It's all free and available at www.ajb.dni.us.

4. Company Profile

The company profile (or the company's one-minute resume, as I like to call it) should always be part of the job posting. A profile should read something like this:

> We are a growing and profitable global $15 billion company with offices spread throughout 71 countries. Founded in 1981 by John Doe, we are headquartered in San Francisco, California, and provide business-to-business computer solutions and Internet and Intranet hosting services.

The company profile should answer these questions at the minimum: who, what, where, and how. Job seekers should know after reading your company profile who you are, what you do, where you do it, and how long you've been doing it. I know this seems basic, but many companies leave out this critical introduction to the company. These questions are important to job seekers and play a major part in whether they want to apply.

You may be wondering, "How do I do this if I have to keep my client company's name confidential?" There is a way you can sell your company without broadcasting its name all over the Internet. You can use generalizations rather than specifics, such as in the following company miniresume:

> We are currently staffing for a Fortune 50 company located in sunny San Jose, California. It is experiencing high growth and looking for key individuals to take charge of its new satellite offices. Very comprehensive benefits and compensation package, hiring bonus, and employee stock options offered . . .

5. Job Description

A detailed, precise, well-thought-out job description will improve your responses by screening out candidates who aren't interested in the job details. What good is having twenty people respond to a job posting if they are not qualified or not interested in your job after hearing more about it? You should paint a clear enough picture so the job seeker gets an idea of the scope and nature of the position, including important tasks and responsibilities (even the unpleasant ones). There is quite a debate about this issue among HR professionals—many feel a job should be glorified and the unpleasant aspects should be hidden at all costs. I'm a firm believer that you need to inform the job seeker of the good, the bad, and the ugly. What are we accomplishing with a great hire that we have to replace after six weeks because he or she couldn't handle the unpleasant duties of the job? What have we done for our image and reputation? My philosophy is that honesty is the best policy. A job description—online or in print—should have as many details as necessary to give the job seeker a pretty good handle on the job's scope.

The increase in responsibilities of the human resource department is becoming more and more apparent. We not only have to find talent, but once we find them, we have to screen, interview, hire, orient, and develop them. We are frequently stretched to our limit, and some of us just don't take the extra time to write job descriptions or keep them up to date. Hopefully, after reading this section, you will be convinced that you need to devote special attention to this area.

Following is a checklist of the items you may want to include in your job description.

1. Status: State whether the position is full time, contract, per diem, exempt or nonexempt, etc.
2. Hours (day shift, trick work, etc.)
3. Percentage of travel required
4. Position summary with list of major duties and responsibilities
5. Supervisory or managerial responsibilities
6. Skills or proficiencies
7. Functional reporting or departmental information
8. Language skills required
9. Physical demands (if any—be careful not to discriminate against the disabled)
10. Equipment/computer systems used in the job

Note: Some job banks have separate category boxes to include this information. In such cases, you do not have to repeat this information in the job description.

Have you ever been given a job requisition for a newly created job in your company and not had a clue as to how to write the job description or the qualifications required? All you got from the hiring manager was a two-line blurb specifying the preferred degree and two years' experience working with widgets. This is a common problem for HR professionals. If you're having any difficulty with a job analysis for a new position, don't fret. Look at the next section. There are companies and online web sites that offer comprehensive instructions and complete job summaries for whatever job description you may have to write.

Job Descriptions Now (www.jobdescriptions.com) provides comprehensive job descriptions, complete with specific responsibilities of the job and ADA compliance requirements. What can you expect to pay for such a service? For a single use, under $10.00; for a three-month subscription with unlimited use, $49.95; and for a twelve-month unlimited-use subscription, $89.95. (These prices were in effect in January 1999 and are subject to change.) From the sample in Figure 1, you can see how extensive their job descriptions are. This description includes such details as physical demands and reasoning ability. How many of your job descriptions are this detailed? I'm not recommending that you post all the information shown in Figure 1 online. However, this site provides the framework for a particular job description and allows for easy modifications to fit your own unique requirements. This site is especially helpful when you are in the job analysis stage of developing a new job.

6. Job Specifications

Job specifications are the minimum acceptable qualifications, skills, and proficiencies the candidate should possess in order to perform the job. If three years' supervisory experience is a requirement of the job, you should say so in the job posting. Most HR professionals know the importance of specifying job-related criteria in a job description. There is even greater reason to do so when you are online—first, you have the space available at no additional cost, and second, specifications help candidates screen themselves out of jobs they are not capable of performing. So make sure you have accurate data from hiring managers and that you are using the most current specifications of the job being performed. This is especially true for newly created jobs or jobs that have changed over the years but haven't had an appropriate job evaluation or analysis performed.

7. Education Level Required

Education level is actually a part of the job specifications, but it is listed separately here for two very good reasons. One reason is that most online job boards list education as a separate category. The second reason is that inclusion of the required education level either reduces or increases the candidate pool. For example, in your geographic area, if you don't have many degreed professionals in the labor market and you post a college degree requirement to a local job board, how many responses do you think you'll receive? Specifying education level in the job posting is necessary. If you're posting for a chemical engineering position, you may

FIGURE 1. SAMPLE JOB DESCRIPTION FROM JOB DESCRIPTIONS NOW

>> Job Title: **Marketing Manager**

>> Department: **Marketing**

>> Reports to: **President**

>> FLSA Status: **Nonexempt**

>> Summary: **Plans, directs, and coordinates the marketing of the organization's products and/or services by performing the following duties personally or through subordinate supervisors.**

Essential duties and responsibilities include the following. Establishes marketing goals to ensure share of market and profitability of products and/or services. Other duties may be assigned.

Develops and executes marketing plans and programs, both short- and long-range, to ensure profit growth and expansion of company products and/or services.

Researches, analyzes, and monitors financial, technological, and demographic factors so that market opportunities may be capitalized on and the effects of competitive activity may be minimized.

Plans and oversees the organization's advertising and promotion activities including print, electronic, and direct mail outlets. Communicates with outside advertising agencies on ongoing campaigns. Works with writers and artists and oversees copywriting, design, layout, pasteup, and production of promotional materials.

Develops and recommends pricing strategy for the organization, which will result in the greatest share of the market over the long run. Achieves satisfactory profit/loss ratio and share of market performance in relation to preset standards and to general and specific trends within the industry and the economy.

Ensures effective control of marketing results and sees that corrective action takes place to be certain that the achievement of marketing objectives is within designated budgets.

Evaluates market reactions to advertising programs, merchandising policy, and product packaging and formulation to ensure the timely adjustment of marketing strategy and plans to meet changing market and competitive conditions.

Recommends changes in basic structure and organization of marketing group to ensure the effective fulfillment of objectives assigned to it and provide the flexibility to move swiftly in relation to marketing problems and opportunities.

Conducts marketing surveys on current and new product concepts. Prepares marketing activity reports.

>> Supervisory Responsibilities: **Manages three subordinate supervisors who supervise a total of five employees in the Marketing Department. Is responsible for the overall direction, coordination, and evaluation of this unit. Also directly supervises two nonsupervisory employees. Carries out supervisory responsibilities in accordance with the organization's policies and applicable laws. Responsibilities include interviewing, hiring, and training employees; planning, assigning, and directing work; appraising performance; rewarding and disciplining employees; addressing complaints; and resolving problems.**

>> Qualifications: **To perform this job successfully, an individual must be able to perform each essential duty satisfactorily. The requirements listed below are representative of the knowledge, skills, and/or ability required. Reasonable accommodations may be made to enable individuals with disabilities to perform the essential functions.**

>> Education and/or Experience: **Master's degree (M.A.) or equivalent; or 4 to 10 years' related experience and/or training; or equivalent combination of education and experience.**

>> Language Skills: **Ability to read, analyze, and interpret common scientific and technical journals, financial reports, and legal documents. Ability to respond to common inquiries or complaints from customers, regulatory agencies, or members of the business community. Ability to write speeches and articles for publication that conform to prescribed style and format. Ability to effectively present information to top management, public groups, and/or boards of directors.**

>> Mathematical Skills: **Ability to apply advanced mathematical concepts such as exponents, logarithms, quadratic equations, and permutations. Ability to apply**

mathematical operations to such tasks as frequency distribution, determination of test reliability and validity, analysis of variance, correlation techniques, sampling theory, and factor analysis.

>> Reasoning Ability: **Ability to define problems, collect data, establish facts, and draw valid conclusions. Ability to interpret an extensive variety of technical instructions in mathematical or diagram form and deal with several abstract and concrete variables.**

>> Physical Demands: **The physical demands described here are representative of those that must be met by an employee to successfully perform the essential functions of this job. Reasonable accommodations may be made to enable individuals with disabilities to perform the essential functions. While performing the duties of this job, the employee is regularly required to sit and talk or hear. The employee frequently is required to use hands to finger, handle, or feel. The employee is occasionally required to stand, walk, and reach with hands and arms.**

have to require a college degree; however, you should not just arbitrarily post college degree requirements if they aren't absolutely necessary. Did you know that Steve Jobs, the cofounder of Apple Computer, didn't finish his degree? I'm sure there are many other successful CEOs and very talented people without a college degree. If you specify a degree requirement in your job posting, you are automatically eliminating a number of possible candidates who may be as qualified as Steve Jobs. This issue is debatable, and many companies want only the top 1 percent of graduating college students to join their staff. When you put the word *required* next to a specified degree, you automatically reduce your candidate pool by thousands of potential candidates who may have exceptional work experience and be capable of doing the job. Take a hard look at the possibility of substituting related work experience for education level or at least "preferred" for "required" education level.

Additionally, on a legal note, having strict employment practices (for example, not considering any candidates who do not have a high school diploma or a college degree) could land you in court facing an Equal Employment Opportunity Commission (EEOC) violation. One such lawsuit was Griggs vs. Duke Power Company. The court sided with Griggs, a black man who applied for a job as coal handler with Duke Power. He was rejected because he did not have a high school diploma. The court ruled that the burden of proof that a hiring standard is job related is on the employer. The employment practice (such as requiring a high school diploma) must be shown to be related to job performance. In this case, the court concluded that Duke's educational requirements had an adverse impact on the minority population even though the company didn't intentionally discriminate.

8. Location

Job seekers normally will not respond to an online job posting if location is not specified or if just general vicinity is mentioned. If you are recruiting for Boston, Massachusetts, you should state Boston rather than "New England states." Even if you have several positions throughout New England, you should specify town, city, and state to achieve better results.

You are also wise to include your policy regarding relocation allowance or visa sponsorships. If your company does not pay relocation or visa sponsorships, and you want to reduce the number of out-of-state/sponsorship resumes, type "No relocation or visa sponsorship" at the beginning of your job description. This will save job seekers time and they won't have to read the entire job details only to be disappointed at the end if you offer no relocation or sponsorship. Remember that Pandora's box is wide open and you may need to put the lid down just a little to keep the resume flow to manageable proportions.

9. Benefits

At the end of this chapter are some samples of job postings that have the characteristics and wording to work for most locations around the globe. However, you may be in a unique situation where you need to be a little more creative, especially to entice the "in-demand" candidates. You may need to dangle some pretty tasty-looking carrots in front of them in order to get their attention. What kinds of carrots are "in-demand" candidates looking for? Besides being highly paid and coddled with a window view, private office, and oak desk, they seem to value flexible work schedules. It's not uncommon to have a systems person (who you know is all hooked up at home) ask to work from home at least one day per week. This trend is becoming more popular with so many people getting wired to electronic gadgets at home. It is not only attractive to the computer techies; office administrators, financial folks, managers, salespeople, and individuals in just about every other profession would like to have some work-at-home flexibility. If your company doesn't offer telecommuting options or flexible work schedules, it should. I'll bet your leading competitor offers some form of flexible schedules or telecommuting benefits.

More women than ever before are in the workforce today. Fathers and mothers want job flexibility to spend more quality time with their families. To attract more women to your company, start reading magazines geared toward this population, such as *Working Mother* or other trade journals. You need to know the wonderful rainbow of diversity of your target audience—men and women, people of color, old and young. Take some mental notes when you interview job seekers. Invest in some surveys (phone, mail, formal, informal, whatever) to find out as much as you can about the people you're targeting to work for your company. Do you need engineers? What type of engineers? What are your competitors offering as starting salaries for recent college graduates? What are some of the key characteristics they seem to be most interested in? Every company will have different questions and answers depending on a wide range of variables—your location, type of industry, and specific business. For example, if you are located in California and are a high-tech start-up company, you are probably in competition for the critical "in-demand" job seekers. What perks and benefits do you need to offer to entice them? You may find out that you need to offer sign-on bonuses, flexible telecommuting arrangements, and/or lucrative stock options to get their attention. On the other hand, if your job opening is in Hickston, Arkansas, you may need to attract your job seekers with a very different tactic and special fishing lures. Get my point? This is just the tip of the iceberg. You need to keep asking questions until you know what job seekers want before they know it themselves.

Whatever the case may be, companies need to be looking long and hard at their internal benefits structures—wage and nonfinancial rewards. In order to compete now and in the future you need to be attracting the best and brightest talent. You need to offer as many benefits as you can think of to potential candidates. You may not be able to increase salary ranges, but there are other benefits you can investigate to make your company more attractive. Leading companies are becoming very innovative in this area by offering flexible scheduling, job sharing, telecommuting, and on-site career counseling. Some companies are even hiring on-site personal service contractors to pick up dry cleaning, or to come to the company's parking lot to wash employees' cars, or even change the oil. These conveniences show how far companies will go to make the working environment pleasant and to allow employees more free time with their families. Successful companies are keeping a watchful eye on the pulse of their workforce and are offering innovative nonfinancial rewards and benefits.

10. Contact Information

The key here is the more the merrier. You should provide as many contacts, phone numbers, fax numbers, web addresses, and e-mail addresses as possible to make it easy for job seekers to respond to your ad. Included within the contact information, you should also code your job postings (online and offline) to track your results and response rates. The easier you make it for the job seeker to respond, the better your chances are to receive more responses. Some job seekers like to send their resume via e-mail, and others do not. Some have access to a fax machine, some don't. Others may find it difficult to contact you via phone since they are working and don't want their current employer to catch them on the phone talking to a recruiter. So give the job seeker as many choices as possible. The most popular method is to have an option for job seekers to apply online after they've read the posting (the trick here is to get them to respond before they click onto another job and forget all about yours). Remember the passive job seekers? They may not have an updated resume on hand. Make sure you have an option for someone to just leave a name and phone number or e-mail address.

JOB SEARCH ENGINE

Job Search Engine, located online at www.jobsearchengine.com, is another option to help your job posting stand out in the crowd of millions. This nifty site allows you to search multiple job sites with one search. You can query CareerMosaic, Headhunter, Monster.com, Yahoo Classifieds, and many more—all at the same time. You search by key word and location and receive a list of jobs found on each site. You can then visit the individual jobs on the list by clicking on the appropriate site. You can use this search engine in several ways. You can see how many other jobs you're competing with. You can see what your competitors are saying to attract job seekers. This is also an excellent method to help you consider which site you want to post your job openings to. For example, if you type in the words *Systems Analyst* you can quickly find out the sites with the most similar jobs in your geographic area.

You may think differently than I do on this subject and believe less is better. Some recruiters would rather compete with fifty openings than five hundred openings because they think their job has a better chance to be seen. In my opinion, more is better. All niche sites and most major commercial sites make it their business to attract the specific disciplines of people they need. I firmly believe the quality and quantity of candidates will be better if you concentrate on sites that are focusing on your specific hiring heeds. You can expect good results from well-known, established niche sites such as Computer Jobs Store, America's Job Bank, Dice Hi-Tech Jobs Online, and Monster.com because they all have the audience of technical people you're looking for. The people at Job Search Engine have a mission—to focus their mega-search engine on high-tech online career opportunities without competing against other products and services. They want to become the indispensable entry point for the high-tech Internet job seeker. I think their mission statement is commendable and definitely helps the job seeker and the recruiter.

Timesaving Techniques

Now that you have learned how to make your job postings stand out in the crowd, let's look at ways you can make the job posting process a little simpler and less time consuming.

SAVING JOB ORDERS AS SHELL DOCUMENTS

You may be thinking, "I don't have time to include all that information in my job postings or to go into that much detail." Or you may be staffing for

FIGURE 2. SAMPLE SHELL DOCUMENT

>> Mission Statement or Company Profile: **We are a staffing company with our first priority on you and your career. If you are looking for a challenging career in the Information Technology field, we want to talk to you. We are currently staffing for a global Fortune 50 company in Rochester, NY, and for various positions across the U.S. This company was rated as one of the top 100 companies to work for in America and has been in existence for over 25 years. We offer excellent wages, benefits, and a fun place to work where your hard work is recognized and rewarded.**

Permanent full-time positions in Rochester are as follows:

>> Contact Information:

Careers R Us
Your Career is "R" business!
1320 Buffalo Road, Suite 203
Rochester, New York 14624
Phone: 716.328.4788
Fax: 716.328.5539
e-mail: dgraham1@rochester.rr.com
Apply online at: Web: frontiernet.net/~careersr
Please reference Job Code #

another firm and lack some of the information you need. One way you can save time and become more efficient is by using shell documents. I call them shells because they are like an outside shell that contains standard headings, closings, company profiles and addresses, phone numbers, fax numbers, e-mail addresses, and other information that doesn't change. Shell documents work well with online recruiting, too. Figure 2 is an example of a standard shell document you can save in a word processing file and use over and over again without retyping. You can copy and paste a "company one-minute resume" and standard contact information. You can have a little information or a lot in your shell documents. You might also want to save all your job descriptions in a separate file in order to do the same thing (copy and paste job descriptions) rather than retype them online every time. All word processing programs have some type of copy-and-paste feature that really comes in handy when you're posting numerous jobs. I recommend including a bit about your company's size, history, standing, and so on.

This advice may seem rudimentary, but I've run across many HR managers and recruiters who don't use this easy technique. Once you get used to using shells, you'll cut your input down to less than half the work. When I see a two-line job posting, I know the recruiter is not using this method or thinking about how much time is really being lost. The little effort and time you take now will save you many hours later on. Whenever you are rekeying a job description ask yourself, "Are these data available somewhere else?" They may be in digital format, on diskette, on someone else's computer, or in hard-copy format. If you receive your job orders by fax or other hard-copy format, you can invest in a nifty piece of software that magically transforms paper into PC documents without retyping them. You can use this software to scan in resumes or job orders received by mail or fax so you don't have to retype the information. Textbridge software products provide scanning technology starting at less than $100. Their web address is www.textbridege.com.

CROSS-POSTING SERVICES

Another timesaving technique is a cross-posting service. Cross posting allows you to minimize your recruitment costs by posting once to receive wider online exposure. You have some choices regarding where you want to post your job openings. Usenets, job boards, and corporate web sites are among them. Usually people join a specific Usenet group according to their individual interests. They can exchange messages publicly or privately and post questions or announcements that may be of interest to the group. Usenets have been a popular place to post job postings.

The benefits of cross-posting services are maximum exposure on leading sites and saving data entry time. How you decide to use the service is really your prerogative. They all work basically the same way—you post your jobs once and the administrators of the site automatically forward (or download) them to other sites. Some services partner with major sites such as Yahoo or Headhunter and others partner with local or niche sites. This is the true power of diversification. The downside to this wonderful software achievement is mainly a problem for job seekers, who are starting to complain because they see the same jobs posted on several different sites. Rather than having 2 million jobs to search, we now have 100 million—and many are duplicate postings. This is more of a nuisance than a major problem since the search capabilities on the Internet allow us to quickly narrow our search results to just the postings we want to investigate. The same is true for resumes—these too are duplicated and we don't want to waste time pulling up the same resumes we already found in another job bank. There is as yet no way to screen out duplicate job postings or resumes. However, by utilizing the best sites offering cross-posting services, the recruiter and the job seeker can search only *one* job site and be relatively assured that they have tapped into the most jobs or resumes.

In the next few years, I estimate all sites will probably offer some type of cross-posting service simply because there are just too many sites competing with each other. I'm afraid that, once again, you will have a wide range of choices and services to choose from. For more information and for vendors providing this service, look at the section in Chapter 4 titled "Let the Software Do the Work."

Legal Aspects of Electronic Recruiting and Job Postings

Now I'd like to discuss a topic that can be uncomfortable and that is sometimes overlooked by the staffing industry—legal aspects of recruiting. The code of conduct for online advertisements is the same as for newspaper advertisements. Discriminating against any age, gender, disability, race, or religious affiliation is as illegal online as it is in print media. Actually, you should be even more careful with online job postings because you are more likely to reach a more diverse audience. So make every effort to be sensitive to the people reading your advertisements. It is just as easy to end up in court with a blatantly discriminatory online job posting as with a newspaper ad.

No Internet police or Affirmative Action Coalition investigates online job ads for any abuses, so it is up to you and your staff to ensure that you are complying with all applicable laws, projecting a favorable corporate image, and providing equal opportunity for all. Improper language in a job posting can often contribute to a lawsuit as a form of "prima facie" (implied or giving the appearance of guilt) evidence. I'm sure you don't want your job advertisement used as evidence in a court of law or even interpreted to be discriminatory, so here are some quick tips to follow.

1. Never make reference to age, even indirectly. Avoid words such as *recent graduate*, *youthful*, and *energetic*. These adjectives can easily be interpreted as being age discriminatory.

2. Be sure not to use gender-specific language, such as the "right man for the job," "foreman," or "repairman." I heard of a legal issue because a job advertisement stated "you must provide your own tuxedo." This advertisement was intentionally targeting men, but by mentioning a male-specific piece of clothing it was discriminating against women.

3. This also applies to people with disabilities. You must remember to not make statements such as "required to stand all day." By using those words you discriminate against people in a wheel-chair who are capable of doing the job. The Americans with Disabilities Act requires employers to make "reasonable accommodation" for people with disabilities.

4. Some employers actually mention in their job postings that they prefer a specific nationality, such as "looking for a sales representative, preferably Japanese or fluent in the Japanese language." The occupational qualification for the job may mandate this requirement, but you are still asking for trouble by stating this in your job posting. While it is okay and perfectly legal to specify in a job description "fluent in the Japanese language," you should avoid the wording "preferably Japanese" or any mention of nationality. Many people of many different origins can speak Japanese. The key is to specify job qualifications rather than nationality. It is always best to leave out any reference to national origin, sex, age, religion, or capabilities. You can always ask specifics during the interview and screening process.

5. To consistently convey an equitable company image, always use the tag line in print and online: "We are an Equal Opportunity Employer" or the customary designation: "EOE M/F/V/D."

Help with H-1B Specialty Occupation Visas

Many companies are in critical need in highly specialized fields, with many positions going unfilled year after year. The positions are empty because there are just not enough skilled people with the education and experience

---

FIGURE 3. SAMPLE ONLINE WORK VISA REQUIREMENTS

Requirements H-1B Specialty Occupation Visas

>> Purpose: Temporary employment for degreed (or equivalent) aliens in professional or specialty occupations.

>> Length of Stay: Initial entry: 3 years; Maximum period of stay: 6 years.

>> Permitted Activities: Productive employment in the United States in a professional job; spouse and children may attend school.

>> Restrictions: No other work in United States allowed. Labor Condition Application must be filed prior to submission of petition. Employee normally needs at least a bachelor's degree to qualify.

---

necessary to fill these openings. Looking outside of our national boundaries can be a costly and complicated alternative. Attorneys' fees can range from hundreds to thousands of dollars to sponsor just one individual. For help in this area you can turn to two great places online. You can download complete step-by-step instructions from a link on Nationjob, located at www.nationjob.com. Another place you might want to check out is Immigration Help Online located at www.immigrationhelp.com/visa.htm. This excellent resource can help you through some of the legal processes, paperwork, and other steps toward hiring individuals with visas. Figure 3 shows the type of information that can be obtained from Immigration Help Online.

Examples of Successful Job Orders

Note that well-written job postings highlight all the components mentioned earlier in this chapter as well as various other advantages of working for the company. The key here is to sell, sell, sell. Following are samples of well-written job postings, complete with key components required to receive a high response rate.

FIGURE 4. SAMPLE PROGRAM MANAGER POSTING

>> Job Title: **Program Manager—Information Technology**

>> Category/Key Words: **Management, Manager, SQL, IT, OLAP, Finance, Consulting, Economics, Microsoft MSF, Windows 95, NT**

>> Company Profile: **Smell the ocean breeze! We are a leading provider of high-performance e-customer solutions for enterprises moving to the web. Headquartered in Santa Monica, California, we have a proven heritage of customer relationship management. We've been a builder of customer-facing applications since 1992. Our focus on the e-customer is a natural extension of our product development, experience, and philosophy. We help companies sell, support, and service customers however they access your enterprise— through call centers, sales reps, field service reps, or web self-service. Our approach means companies don't need to reinvent the IT wheel to serve the e-customer.**

>> Job Description: **Are you looking for a new opportunity with a dynamic, market-leading, creative, and fun organization? This is where your professional goals can be met within a rewarding, intellectually stimulating atmosphere. We are growing and have the following Program Manager full-time permanent position available. Responsibilities include:**

You will work with a small team of highly motivated professionals to deliver an innovative suite of decision support, OLAP applications utilizing the latest technology. The Program Manager position requires a sophisticated mix of business expertise, including translation of client needs into detailed software functional specifications, overall responsibility for managing the development schedule, and assurance that the product suite meets the defined business needs of the clients.

Create and monitor project plans with interfunctional teams (teams include engineering, QA, technical writing, training, technical support, product management, sales, etc.).

Identify and resolve problems hindering release schedule.

Define pre-requirements and packaging.

Release media to fulfillment for duplication.

Provide status reports and configuration updates to the field on a weekly basis.

Update field on long-term plans for database, platform, and client compatible releases.

Work with product managers to ensure that new requirements and enhancements are implemented in plans.

>> Job Specifications: Minimum 3 years' industry experience. As a **Program Manager,** consulting or support capacity w/decision support and/or OLAP applications. **Experience with MSF (Microsoft Solutions Framework) a plus. Also required: good working knowledge of MS Office, Win 95 and NT,** relational databases, SQL. **Must possess excellent communication skills with developers and users.**

Additional Qualifications: Understanding of database application development. Familiarity with operating systems, clients, and software compatibility issues. Excellent track record of releasing the highest possible quality product on time. Excellent problem analysis and problem-solving skills.

>> Education: **B.S. in business, finance, economics, or computer science (preferred). May substitute closely related work experience for degree.**

>> Salary: **75–90K depending on experience**

>> Location: **Santa Monica, CA**

>> Benefits: **HIRING BONUS PAID**

Excellent benefits including comprehensive healthcare plan, 401K, tuition reimbursement, employee stock ownership, flexible schedules, relocation paid

>> Contact Information:

Name: John Doe

Phone: 1.800.xxx.xxxx or 1.333.xxx.xxxx

Address: 55 Employer Street, Santa Monica, CA 90222

Reference Job Code: 1H003

Fax: 1.800.xxx.xxxx or 1.333.xxx.xxxx

Email: johndoe@email.com

Web: www.ABC.com

FIGURE 5. SAMPLE SENIOR SALES EXECUTIVE POSTING

>> Job Title: Sr. Sales Executive

>> Category/Key Words: Customer Care, Consulting, Systems, Software, Customer Service, Call Center

>> Company Profile: Our client is one of the most exciting start-ups that we have represented! It is charting a course to establish itself as the leading consulting and systems integrator in the growing market for Customer Care software and services, a market that's projected to grow from $3.2 billion per year to $10.7 billion per year by 2002, according to the Gartner Group! Customer Care encompasses front office applications such as Sales Force Automation, Customer Support, Marketing, Field Service & Sales Automation, and Call Centers. If you are interested in a well-funded start-up with a relaxed and fun environment, this is the place for you. The potential is here. Come grow with a dynamic, energetic group that believes in their company and its products.

>> Job Description: Exciting opportunity for experienced hands-on marketing person. In this full-time senior-level management position you will be responsible for developing business by delivering customer service. Leading the sales and service staff (10-15 employees), you will manage the recruitment and development of internal staff and develop a local client base. You will use your superior customer service skills to present power presentations to customers and potential new businesses.

>> Job Specifications: Minimum of 2 years' consulting (service—not product) sales experience. Best candidates will bring successful expertise in technology consulting, having been responsible for both project delivery and business development. They will have demonstrated competency in leading and motivating technology consulting teams and developing strong relationship with clients.

Serious candidates will bring a network of contacts within the Boston area, which could potentially yield clients within a relatively short time frame.

>> Education: Two-year college degree, four-year degree a plus.

>> Salary: **75–90K (depending on experience) base pay, plus lucrative commission plan**

>> Location: **Boston, MA**

>> Benefits: **Your benefit package has been designed to provide you and your family with protection in the event of illness, injury, or death, as well as to help provide for your retirement. Medical, dental, vision, life/AD&D, 401K, and employee assistance program become effective upon your date of hire. Short- and long-term disability plans become effective upon your completing 90 days of service. Paid tuition, car allowance, and employee stock ownership plan.**

>> Contact Information:
    Name: John Doe
    Phone: 1.800.xxx.xxxx or 1.xxx.xxx.xxx
    Address: 55 Employer Street, Boston, MA 90222
    Reference Job Code: IH003
    Fax: 1.800.xxx.xxxx or 1.333.xxx.xxx
    Email: Johndoe@email.com
    Web: www.ABC.com

FIGURE 6. SAMPLE REGIONAL DIRECTOR POSTING

>> Job Title: **Regional Director**

>> Category/Key Words: **E-commerce, consulting, consultant, manager, management, director, enterprise, project management**

>> Company Profile: **Our client is a systems-integration consulting firm, founded in 1996 by a well-known high-tech entrepreneur. The previous company he established was made public in 1996 and is now traded on NASDAQ.**

The company offers a wide range of services including custom software development, systems integration, package implementation, Y2K, Internet, and E-commerce solutions consulting. The client has over 200 employees and expects to go public within 10 months.

>> Job Description: **The Regional Director will be responsible for selecting an office site, managing the recruitment and development of internal staff, and developing a local client base, eventually expanding it to include the greater New England region.**

The Regional Director will establish the market's strategic direction and maintain quality control of consulting deliverables, ensuring excellent client relationships:

40% Works with Business Executives and Managers.

20% Manages Staff, including recruitment, training, and development.

20% Develops and improves rigorous systems-life-cycle methodologies appropriate to different platforms/technologies.

10% Serves as a strategic resource to the corporation, including assessment of new technologies.

10% Pursues rigorous program of self-development, including membership in a professional society, establishing and maintaining a network of peers, reviewing technologies and business periodicals, etc. Pursues continuous quality improvement.

Also responsible for coordinating the training of our sales force in our 22 operating cities to include development of new training documents, products, features, and network tools.

>> Job Specifications: **Minimum 5 years' related work experience, at least 2 years of which have been as a senior manager or senior consultant. Demonstrated expertise in enterprise-level project management. Solid understanding of market strategies, system life cycles, and business-to-business consulting practices.**

Familiar with client/server environments, including analysis, programming, and testing disciplines. Business orientation, with excellent written and oral communication skills. Ability to explain technical concepts to a nontechnical audience.

>> Education: Two-year college degree, four-year degree preferred.

>> Salary: 75–90K (depending on experience) base pay, plus lucrative commission plan

>> Location: Boston, MA

>> Benefits: In addition to a superior compensation package, we offer superior benefits! We take pride in our accomplishments and offer our people a comprehensive salary/benefit package that includes medical/dental/vision, paid holidays and vacations, matching 401K, training, pre-tax childcare, std/ltd life insurance.

>> Contact Information:
    Name: John Doe
    Phone: 1.800.xxx.xxxx or 1.333.xxx.xxx
    Address: 55 Employer Street, Boston, MA OH 55333
    Reference Job Code: IH003
    Fax: 1.800.xxx.xxxx or 1.333.xxx.xxx
    Email: Johndoe@email.com

FIGURE 7. SAMPLE SENIOR ORACLE DBA POSTING

>> Job Title: Senior Oracle DBA

>> Category/Key Words: Management, Manager, DBA, Oracle 7, SQL92, PL/SQL, Tune SQL, Java, C++, HTML, Windows NT, SQLNET, Perl

>> Company Profile: Major securities firm located in Sunnyvale, California, seeking Senior Oracle DBA; Hiring bonus paid.

>> Job Description: **Responsible for configuration and maintenance activities and database administration of Oracle 7 database, physical database design, and data structure.**
>
> **Use Oracle tools to monitor and tune databases.**
>
> **Use SQL/plsql. Shell scripting using PERL.**
>
> **Support front end & reports developers. Support Web applications development.**
>
> **Support C++ developers in creating stored procedures, triggers, and data objects.**
>
> **Manage resources on NT server.**

>> Job Specification: **Oracle 7 a must. Oracle 8 preferred. SQL92, PL/SQL, Tune SQL. Use triggers, stored procedures, parallel query, case tools; generate database objects. Database connectivity from Web-based tools, HTML, JAVA. Monitor database, tune database. Windows NT server. SQLNET. Requirements:**
>
> **4 years plus experience**
>
> **Strong communication skills**
>
> **Must have experience in financial industry**
>
> **Database administration of Oracle 7 and Oracle 8 databases**
>
> **Test database applications and assist in application releases**
>
> **Required education: four-year degree**

>> Education: **B.S. in business, finance, economics, or computer science (preferred). May substitute closely related work experience for degree.**

>> Salary: **90–120K depending on experience**

>> Location: **Santa Monica, CA**

>> Benefits: **HIRING BONUS PAID**
Excellent benefits including comprehensive healthcare plan, 401k, tuition reimbursement, employee stock ownership, flexible schedules, relocation paid.

>> Contact Information:

Name: John Doe

Phone: 1.800.xxx.xxxx or 1.333.xxx.xxx

Address: 55 Employer Street, Santa Monica, CA 90222

Reference Job Code: IH003

Fax: 1.800.xxx.xxxx or 1.333.xxx.xxx

Email: Johndoe@email.com

Web: www.ABC.com

FIGURE 8. NATIONAL CALL CENTER MANAGER POSTING

>> Job Title: National Call Center Manager

>> Key Words: call center, manager, management, project, help desk, GTS, customer service

>> Company Profile: Come to the beautiful Finger Lakes! We are located in the heart of the beautiful Finger Lakes region. We are currently seeking a National Call Center Manager to be responsible for the operational functions of the Solutions Center covering upstate New York, including Buffalo, Rochester, and Syracuse. We have been in business since 1973 and are growing at a rate of 15% per year. In the last three years we have registered double-digit sales and profit growth. We have a 45% share of the telecommunications market totaling sales over $15 million.

>> Job Description: This full-time position as a Call Center Manager oversees all operational functions of the Solutions Center organization, including staff/leadership development, day-to-day management, project involvement, and client/vendor relationships. Facilitates the recruitment, appraisal, and development of Analysts, Specialists, Senior Specialists, Team Leaders, and Lead IT Experts.

Performs real-time analysis of IT issues. Gathers, interprets, and integrates data from diverse sources for resolution of problems, reports, special projects, and/or presentations. Maintains own technical proficiency through conferences, technical seminars, and other learning activities. Project Involvement: Approves Solutions Center technical support of GTS initiatives. Demonstrates knowledge of applications, platforms, and trends of technology currently utilized by the Firm. Delegates projects to team, based on knowledge of the client's needs and staff's skill set. Client/Vendor Relationships: Interfaces proactively with people in all business units and at all levels of the Firm, representing the Solutions Center's mission and policies. Consults with outside vendors in resolution of problems, contract terms, and product evaluations.

Instills sense of ownership, initiative, and enthusiasm in Solutions Center staff, counseling and coaching employees when necessary on personnel issues. Measures staff's performance and morale. Monitors Skills-Based Management process. Implements forecasting and scheduling process and tools. Briefs the staff on project developments, vision, and strategies. Operations: Leads development of customer support strategy and scope definition for the Solutions Center. Responsible for the Solutions Center's continuous improvement efforts in the areas of Operations and Knowledge Management.

Responsible for tactical operations of Solutions Center site and facilities. Evaluates new technologies to improve Solutions Center operations and processes. Develops and administers Solutions Center procedures with appropriate quality controls. Support 50,000 end users.

>> Job Specifications: 5 to 10 years' corporate experience in a similar Information Technology or Support Services environment. Prior management experience required. Prior Help Desk or Call Center experience required. Excellent verbal, written, presentation, and communication skills with a strong client service orientation. Thorough and detail oriented with good administrative, financial, and organizational skills.

>> Education: A bachelor's degree in computer science, information technology, business, or equivalent education preferred.

>> Salary: 65–75K depending on experience

>> Location: Cleveland, OH

>> Benefits: In addition to a superior compensation package, we offer superior benefits! We take pride in our accomplishments and offer our people a comprehensive salary/ benefit package that includes medical/dental/vision, paid holidays and vacations, matching 401K, training, pre-tax child care, std/ltd life insurance.

>> Contact Information:
Name: John Doe
Phone: 1.800.xxx.xxxx or 1.333.xxx.xxx
Address: 55 Employer Street, Cleveland, OH 00000
Reference Job Code: IH004
Fax: 1.800.xxx.xxxx or 1.xxx.xxx.xxx
Email: Johndoe@email.com
Web: www.ABC.com

FIGURE 9. TECHNICAL SALES ENGINEER POSTING

>> Job Title: Technical Sales Engineer

>> Key Words: chemical, sales, water treatment, chemical engineering, engineer

>> Company Profile: ABC Company is a recognized global leader in the sales and service of specialty water and process treatment chemicals and chemical feed control systems. Our Global Headquarters is located in Pittsburgh, PA (USA), with global business unit offices located in Europe (Belgium), Asia-Pacific (Singapore), and Latin America (Brazil). Subsidiary and Division offices are located in most countries throughout the world. The business unit headquarters provide support for field sales personnel worldwide.

>> Responsibilities: Utilize your engineering background and your people skills in a fun work environment with a growing high-tech company! We're looking for ambitious engineers with excellent communication skills, strong mechanical aptitudes, and superior

technical problem-solving skills. You will take a proactive approach to solve industrial problems by calling customers and offering solutions aimed at increasing the efficiency, quality, and reliability in our customer's manufacturing plants.

The successful candidate will also be responsible for chemical and specialty water treatment sales for our office headquarters in Pittsburgh, PA. Launch new products, conduct seminars, and assess customer application requirements in a pre-sales role.

>> Job Specifications: At least 2 years' chemical sales experience.

Primary qualification would be water treatment experience and secondary qualification would include outside technical sales experience.

>> Education: B.S. degree in chemical engineering, mechanical engineering, chemistry, or associated technical degree required.

>> Salary: 65–75K depending on experience, plus lucrative commission plan

>> Benefits: We offer a competitive salary and benefits package, including profit sharing, dental, tuition reimbursement, and 401K participation with no waiting period. As an equal opportunity employer, all employment and personnel decisions are based on individual applicant and employee qualifications, skills, and abilities and shall not be made on the basis of age, race, creed, sex, national origin, veteran status, or non-disqualifying disability.

>> Contact Information:

Name: John Doe
Phone: 1.800.xxx.xxxx or 1.333.xxx.xxx
Address: 55 Employer Street, Pittsburgh, PA, OH 00000
Reference Job Code: IH005
Fax: 1.800.xxx.xxxx or 1.xxx.xxx.xxx
Email: Johndoe@email.com
Web: www.ABC.com

To learn more about the way ABC Company is shaping the future of water and process treatment, or to submit your resume, visit our home page at http://www.abc.com.

Below is an example of a common job posting that can be found on any job site at any given time.

Job Posting

Sales Engineer Requirements: **4 Year Degree: At Least 3 Years Experience** Required Travel: **Up to 25%. Contact Joe Recruiter at 305.999.9999. Salary Negotiable.**

So what is wrong with this short job ad? More than likely no one ever bothered to call Joe Recruiter for the following reasons: He forgot to mention where the job is located. He listed just a phone number (online job seekers prefer e-mail and don't want to incur phone charges or bother with playing phone tag). He didn't tell me anything about the job, so why would I even bother when I have so many other jobs online to inquire about? He didn't tell me the type of engineering degree required (that is, mechanical, electrical, industrial). He didn't tell me what product or service I would be helping to sell. He didn't tell me where I would be selling it or where I would be traveling. Most important, he didn't tell me how much I might expect to be paid for selling something I don't have a clue about. I also don't have a clue if I'm even qualified for the position. Compare this job to some of the sample job descriptions just listed.

Let's look at another possible scenario. Let's say, hypothetically, that Joe Recruiter listed a salary range of up to $120,000/year. This could cause Joe to get inundated with phone calls from every sales representative and engineer in the country, inquiring more about this opening. How much time has he saved now? I hope I've made my point—being brief in online recruiting is bad in every possible circumstance. Job seekers expect more information about jobs when they are online. You need to be writing it better and snappier than the other guy is.

In the old days of recruiting, an effective recruiter's main objective was to get to the short list of candidates (that is, the list of truly qualified candidates culled from the list of all applicants). With online recruiting, you should strive to write a more comprehensive job posting and receive only qualified candidates who are ready, willing, and able to consider the position.

Coding

Don't be afraid to experiment and track your results. Always put a code or tracking number within the job postings so you can determine where the job seeker saw your ad. For example, a newspaper advertisement in San Jose could be coded NSJ-N for newspaper and SJ for San Jose. For an online job posting on America's Job Bank, I would use the code IAJB. It doesn't matter what coding system you use, as long as you use some form of tracking mechanism that makes sense to you and your staff. You should also keep a log of the results. Periodically check the responses—discontinue or reduce frequency of less successful sources and increase frequency of the ones that are working best. The numeral at the end of the code refers to the sequence of the ad or posting—for example, the first, second, or third ad appearance or version of the job posting. Following are some examples of easy coding systems.

Source	Code
Newspaper	Dept. NSJ001
Job Fair	JF.Boston002
Online America's Job Bank	Dept. IAJB001
Online Yahoo	Dept. IYH001
Online CareerWeb	Dept. ICW003

In review, whenever you need to write a power job posting, be sure to use the following checklist if you want to ensure getting an optimal response.

- Use the ten key components of job posting.
- Use online help such as Job Descriptions Now.
- Use shell documents or other saved files to save time.
- Follow legal and EEOC guidelines when recruiting online.
- Use a coding system to track results.

KEY CONCEPTS

>> The three most critical areas to focus on to help you improve responses to online job posting are key words, job title, and salary. Audits have shown that job postings that include salary achieve a higher response rate—sometimes three times the rate of response.

>> There are three strategies to increase the odds of your online jobs being seen and responded to.
1. Use the ten key components of online job postings.
2. Make recruitment advertising effective.
3. Choose the best job board(s) to meet your needs.

>> The best-written job description will never be read if it doesn't pop up in the search results because you didn't select the proper category, job titles, and key words.

>> Use the word "management" in key words, titles, or categories to increase responses to job postings.

>> Include a mini company profile—the "company's one-minute resume."

>> Be careful in specifying requirements such as education level. Instead use "preferred" or substitute work experience when feasible to increase your candidate pool.

>> Keep a close eye on what your competitors and other successful companies are doing in the area of benefits and nonfinancial rewards to attract job seekers.

>> Maximize your exposure by utilizing cross-posting services.

Chapter Two

Resume Surfing

Attention recruiters: People for sale to the highest bidder! Human auctions? Has the new century created so great a demand for candidates that we are willing to put a monetary value on human beings? Well, in July 1999 that is exactly what Monster.com advertised it was going to do, and it proceeded to introduce the world's first real-time online auction-style marketplace, called Talent Market. Using this innovative method, job seekers and independent professionals (consultants and independent contractors) don "for sale" signs with the intent of mutually negotiating projects, services, and contracts with employers. Professionals are able to create an online profile to showcase their skills and give employers details regarding their work preferences (geographic location, acceptable salary range, ideal projects, desired length of work they are seeking, and so on).

This new way of recruiting (or should I say "bidding"?) for employees is receiving some well-deserved attention, and a good number of successful placements have been achieved. If this idea of auction-style recruiting doesn't seem appealing to you, you might want to try some other innovative recruiting method such as resume surfing. This chapter will show you how to source, search, and surf the sea of resumes to increase the number of resumes in your qualified candidate pool without any bidding.

You already know there are millions of job postings online, but did you know there are millions of resumes available to you as well? Many estimate that the total number of resumes posted on the web falls somewhere between

20 and 50 million. The Fast Facts table shows the number of resumes online from just three leading sites.

Some companies, such as Hewlett-Packard, design and maintain their own resume data and storage. Hewlett-Packard's sophisticated resume database has technology capable of recognizing many different languages. It can fill vacancies for HP globally and at last check contained over 150,000 resumes. Other companies outsource resume storage to another firm. For example, many major newspapers use iSearch (www.isearch.com) to handle resumes from eighty-eight affiliated newspapers using the Resume Connection. iSearch, creator of Internet-enabled candidate sourcing and applicant tracking tools, has helped some very well known companies (Signal, Raychem, Tribune Company, Nortel Networks, eBay, Fleet Bank, Bay Networks, BellSouth, Intel, Knight-Ridder, Motorola, Texaco, TRW, and Xerox) handle the heavy influx of online resumes. According to Electronic Recruiting Newswire, iSearch announced on May 25, 1999, that it had achieved an industry record for accessible resumes on the Internet with over 3 million active online resumes. And the numbers are growing rapidly. To reduce all these resumes into manageable results, you need to know some strategies for narrowing your candidate pool to only the list of candidates that match your hiring requirements. There are two methods of resume surfing—the pull method and the push method.

Twenty Popular Choices for Job Seekers

The pull method evolved from users searching for data by hunting and pecking through the Internet and the web via search engines. You pull everything you want to you. Then some enterprising souls saw value in pushing data to users based on their preferences. So if you're a sports fan, for example, and like sporting events and scores at your fingertips, push technology can deliver this information with little effort on your part. You simply enter your interests or needs into a server and a database collects all the information it feels is relevant and pushes the data to your desktop. For recruitment, you and job seekers can use the pull method to search resumes and job postings to your heart's content or you can use the push method to have them pushed at you. You can use both methods if you prefer.

For one minute, let's just put on our job seeker's shoes and explore all the options available in our job search tool kit. Using approaches similar to those of the job seeker, we increase the odds of hooking up with each other. In the last decade, job seekers had only a few choices when it came to looking for jobs. They could

1. Look in the employment classified section of their local newspaper or journals
2. Network with friends, relatives, and colleagues
3. Sign up with a recruiter, headhunter, or executive search firm
4. Attend job fairs, canvass directly, and file applications with employers
5. Mass mail their unsolicited resumes with a broad marketing campaign

Today, job seekers have not only these options but many more. Some of the newer and more popular choices are as follows:

6. Attend a virtual job fair online (face-to-face interview via video-conference)
7. Create a virtual resume and post to web page
8. Apply online directly to employer's web site
9. Search jobs online at major, local, and niche recruiting sites and job posting boards
10. Submit resume online to major, local, or niche recruiting sites
11. Submit resume to Usenet(s)
12. Submit resume to select government agencies
13. Submit resume online to a trade organization or an online community
14. Submit resume to a career placement agency or outplacement firm
15. Sign up for automatic e-mail notification of jobs when employers post them
16. Register with resume distribution services
17. Directly canvass recruiters and employers by e-mail
18. Register with a college-affiliated job bank (available to college students and recent graduates)
19. Use a resume bureau search firm
20. Register with a job site or resume bank confidentially

When you look at the options available to job seekers you can clearly see that there are many opportunities for you to capitalize on this new recruiting revolution. You have probably already perfected items 1 through

5 and have been receiving resumes by this method since the beginning of your HR experience. However, items 6 through 20 may appear new or unfamiliar to you. So let's look at each one individually.

ATTEND A VIRTUAL JOB FAIR ONLINE

Online job fairs are a very popular avenue for many companies. The newspaper industry is starting to offer virtual job fairs in addition to traditional job fairs. One that comes to mind, the Westech Virtual Job Fair, has been operating successfully to attract a wide range of highly technical talent, as well as the general public. With the popularity of videoconferencing technology, this method is becoming more attractive to both job seekers and recruiters. The possibility of interviewing (face to face via videoconferencing equipment) many potential candidates in a short period and over long distances is very cost-effective. Colleges are starting to offer virtual job fairs as well. Career placement departments on college campuses usually set up the equipment via a computer, camera, and microphone hooked up to a PC—voila, instant interviews.

CREATE A VIRTUAL RESUME AND POST TO WEB PAGE

Virtual resumes are increasing in popularity. Did you realize many Internet providers are giving their customers free web pages and space? Many job seekers are using this free space to showcase their resumes. There are also many new services that offer the design and placement of resumes online. This means there are also many job seekers available who may not be in a job bank at all. Instead, they may have their resumes posted only to their own personal web pages. As software becomes easier to learn, I see this avenue growing to huge proportions. It has to be more cost-effective to direct an employer or recruiter to a web site (accessible from anywhere in the world) to obtain all the possible information about a potential candidate. This is proving to be a valuable tool for web designers to sell their services. After all, companies are using the web for electronic brochures—why not for job seekers to showcase their talents?

If you would like to check out this valuable source for finding talented people, you can go to any of the search engines, such as AltaVista, and type in "resume.htm." You will usually get about a hundred resumes posted to personal web pages to review. As with most search engines, a short bio of the candidate is listed in the summary results list to help you narrow your search. There is also a web site dedicated to this sourcing of resumes called Flip Search, located at www.flipsearch.com.

APPLY ONLINE DIRECTLY TO EMPLOYER'S WEB SITE

Many companies in a recruiting mode have made it as easy as possible for job seekers to apply for employment. When job seekers are visiting an employer's web site they have an opportunity to enter their information and/or resume into online templates. In a matter of minutes they have applied. If you have listed employment opportunities on a web site, you should offer an e-mail address to click for information or, better yet, allow visitors to submit their resume or information while they're checking out your opportunities. Remember, the passive job seeker may not even have a resume, so you should also have an option for inquiring about a job opening without a resume. In addition, you should have a confidentiality option available so a job seeker can remain anonymous during the inquiry stage and have the option to learn more about a position without revealing his or her identity (see page 73 for more information on confidentiality).

SEARCH JOBS ONLINE AT MAJOR, LOCAL, OR NICHE RECRUITING SITES AND JOB POSTING BOARDS

If you want to be seen when a job seeker is searching online for jobs, you already know you have to use some type of job posting service. You need to carefully choose the recruiting sites that reach your target audience. An entire chapter (Chapter 6) has been devoted to the "where to" so you can make educated and informed decisions rather than just signing up for whatever job posting board you happen to hear about that week.

SUBMIT RESUME ONLINE TO MAJOR, LOCAL, OR NICHE RECRUITING SITES

This is by far the most popular method job seekers are choosing to get their resumes in your hands. Almost all recruitment sites and job boards allow job seekers to submit their resumes to a database for employers to search. Many job seekers are submitting their resumes to multiple boards to maximize their exposure. Many prefer to submit their resumes confidentially, so make sure your recruitment site offers this option. If it doesn't, you may not be receiving the high-quality candidates you are looking for.

SUBMIT RESUME TO USENET(S)

Usenets or newsgroups are user networks that have been popular with the Internet community for a long time. People join special interest user networks to chat with people who share the same interests, to exchange messages publicly or privately, and to post questions or announcements that may be of interest to the group. There are hundreds to choose from. They remain popular places for passive as well as active job seekers to hang out. Electronic notification of resumes hitting the Internet and more information on Usenet groups will be discussed in Chapter 5.

SUBMIT RESUME TO SELECT GOVERNMENT AGENCIES

There are many wonderful agencies (believe it or not) set up and run quite efficiently by the U.S. government. Many of these agencies offer tax incentives and prescreened applicants just for the asking. One such agency is the Unemployment Office operated by the U.S. Department of Labor in every city and state across the country. In Chapter 5, America's Job Bank and the Department of Defense resume database (DORS) are discussed extensively because they both have an enormous talent bank of candidates available for you to search (absolutely free). The Office of Vocational and Educational Services for Individuals with Disabilities (VESID) is another wonderful source of qualified candidates, most of whom have been retrained and all of whom want to work. These candidates come with incentives, such as thousands of dollars in tax credits, on-the-job training (OJT), work tryout, and job coaching.

SUBMIT RESUME ONLINE TO A TRADE ORGANIZATION OR AN ONLINE COMMUNITY

This is a valuable community resource that many companies do not tap into. Trade organizations often offer their members and other job seekers an opportunity to submit their resumes online to a resume bank. You should make sure you know which ones are applicable to your industry and target your searches or post your jobs online with these organizations.

Online communities serve as centers for people who share special interests (very similar to user networks). GeoCities, located at www.geocities.com, is one of the largest and hosts a variety of interests—from golf to government and from fashion to fishing. They are all free and attract people with similar interests. Other trade organizations are the American Society of Metallurgical Engineers (www.asme.org) and the Society for Human Resource Management (SHRM; www.shrm.org). There are hundreds more and they are a great resource to tap into.

SUBMIT RESUME TO A CAREER PLACEMENT AGENCY OR AN OUTPLACEMENT FIRM

Since outplacement firms are hired by companies to find employment for displaced, laid off, or downsized workers, they usually offer a free resume database for employers to search. Generally, the fees are paid by the client company so you have access to some highly skilled, educated, and eager-to-work candidates. One of the largest U.S. outplacement firms that offers a free resume database for employers to search is Drake Beam Morin (www.dbm.com). You can register on the company's web site and start searching for candidates in about twenty seconds.

Besides outplacement firms, just about every community and city has some nonprofit organization offering career development or career transition services. These community-based professional development organizations often have resume databases of local job seekers. They will also yield some very talented and eager-to-work candidates ready for a career change. You can look in the online yellow pages or in the phone book.

SIGN UP FOR AUTOMATIC E-MAIL NOTIFICATION OF JOBS WHEN EMPLOYERS POST THEM

You should definitely consider using a job board that offers this technology to the job seeker. Nationjob (www.nationjob.com) is the pioneer of this automatic e-mail notification system. Many other "automatic scouts" or "automatic agents" have entered the picture as well. They offer job seekers the opportunity to have jobs "pushed" at them via e-mail so they don't have to take the time to search jobs matching their specific interest or job requirements. This service is very attractive to the passive job seeker who may not be thinking seriously about changing jobs but doesn't want to miss out on a great opportunity. Nationjob had over 350,000 subscribers as of June 1999.

REGISTER WITH RESUME DISTRIBUTION SERVICES

Another push method is to register with resume distribution services. Many recruiters and employers allow (and some prefer) job seekers to send an electronic version of their resumes. Many services have sprung up to accommodate and complement this method of recruiting. Resume distribution services charge the job seeker, not the employer or recruiter. This is quite the opposite of most online recruiting services, where the job seeker receives tools and advice absolutely free. All the major sites offer free services to the job seeker—this is how they stay competitive. The revenues are generated from banner advertisements and fees charged to recruiters or employers for posting jobs or searching resumes. So how can a service charge the job seeker? Well, these services are targeted to the serious job seekers, who are paying between $50 and $200 to have their resumes distributed to thousands of recruiters. The concept is great and can save job seekers quite a bit of money by reducing the cost of postage from mass "snail mailings." Job seekers also seem to like the idea of their resumes being exposed to the maximum possible number of recruiters.

There are a couple of caution flags I must wave in front of you before you start doing back flips from excitement. Although some of these candidates are very skilled and high on the employability scale, some are not. Some people may even consider a job seeker who pays to have a resume mass distributed a little on the desperate side. Some may argue that these candidates may be lazy or insufficiently computer savvy to register their resume for free online. However, this problem is not confined to resume distribution services. You will find desperate job seekers and people who are low on the employability scale everywhere. Therefore it is my opinion, in this age of managing the scarcity, that even if only one placement is made per year, these services are worth considering. Since such distribution services are free to employers and recruiters, provider names and web addresses can be obtained from Chapter 5—"The Best of the Freebies."

DIRECTLY CANVASS RECRUITERS AND EMPLOYERS BY E-MAIL

Many savvy job seekers are obtaining e-mail addresses of recruiting firms, staffing agencies, human resource managers, and key individuals at specific companies and e-mailing them their resumes. If you don't have or aren't using an e-mail address in your recruiting efforts, you are definitely at a disadvantage. You should also make sure your e-mail address is registered with online yellow pages and with as many directories as you can find.

REGISTER WITH A COLLEGE-AFFILIATED JOB BANK

Most colleges offer students and recent graduates an option of receiving job placement assistance. The days of students wading through a sea of job openings hand scratched or poorly typed and posted willy-nilly on a college bulletin board are long gone. Instead, they are turning to online job banks such as JobTrak (www.jobtrak.org), which has partnered with over 900 college career placement offices to assist new grads in obtaining employment in their field of study. JobTrak receives over 35,000 visitors and posts 3,000 new job postings each day. If you need new college graduates, check into a college resume bank. Some are listed in the directory of specialty and niche recruiting web sites in Appendix C.

USE A RESUME BUREAU SEARCH FIRM

Many companies are starting to outsource resume searching to firms that specialize in maintaining up-to-date resume databases. One such firm is SkillSearch (www.skillsearch.com), used by Abbott Laboratories, Avon Products, Southwestern Bell, and many other companies. SkillSearch targets recent college graduates and maintains a seven-page member profile, which helps the company selectively match its clients' job requests. For example, if a client is looking for a project manager with three years' experience in electronic manufacturing who is willing to relocate to Boston, the profile will be detailed enough to select only those job seekers matching these unique qualifications. This method of outsourcing resume searching is quite appealing and provides recruiters with a fresh list of available job seekers with a quick turnaround.

REGISTER WITH A JOB SITE OR RESUME BANK CONFIDENTIALLY

Another attractive method, especially to passive job seekers, is the confidential resume. If job seekers are already employed or consulting, the anonymity feature is especially important. Anonymous resume banks have the following features:

- Job seekers can submit a miniresume without having to provide their full name or the name of the company they're currently working for.

- An online template asks just a few questions—ten at the most. Studies have found that a detailed application is too cumbersome—many job seekers won't take the time to complete it if it's too complex or lengthy.
- They provide someone (preferably in the job seeker's field) other than a recruiter to call. High-tech companies are providing online buddies and mentors to develop relationships with potential candidates.
- Job seekers are provided with a way to confidentially inquire about a posting by e-mail or phone (should list an 800 phone number).
- A virtual tour or online company orientation is available where a potential candidate can learn about a company's culture, work climate, benefits, policies, size, locations, and so on.

Using the Pull and Push Methods of Online Recruiting

Let's review all the available pull method options. You can pull resumes toward you from all the places mentioned below.

1. Commercial sites
2. Niche sites
3. Corporate web pages
4. Personal web pages
5. Usenets
6. Online communities
7. Government agencies
8. Trade organizations
9. Outplacement services
10. College placement banks
11. Resume research bureaus

You can also use the following push method choices:

1. Attend virtual job fairs
2. Receive resumes from distribution services
3. Have job seekers submit their resume directly to your database on your corporate web page
4. Receive electronic notification of resumes hitting the Internet or of conversations going on in newsgroups
5. Register your web and e-mail addresses so job seekers can find you on leading search engines and in online directories

Search Engines and Mega Search Tools

As you can see, you have quite a few options available. You need to know how to use all of them effectively and efficiently. To maximize your recruiting efforts, you should use options that are available to both you and the job seeker. Information is the key and the master locksmiths are the search engines. With so much information, so little time, so many choices, and so much confusion, my guiding principle has always been to KISS all this stuff. KISS is the acronym for "keep it simple, stupid." I try to keep my online strategies as simple as I can. My background isn't in computer science, and if you're reading this book I doubt yours is, so why be bothered with all the computer-geek stuff if we don't need it? If you don't want to become a master in search criteria, use the profusion of free services to help you search many different search engines at the same time.

Searching varies a bit among different search engines and databases. You just need to familiarize yourself with a particular site's search logic. Most sites have a help or search button and tips to help you with the options. Once you are used to one, the rest are so similar that you will become a search wizard before you know it. If you enjoy searching the Internet for information, you'll really appreciate improving your searching skills. There are many shortcuts as well as poor online habits. Have you found yourself in the habit of repeating a search on different search engines (or the same one) until you get the results you want? Well, here is a little trick you may find helpful. You may not have the time or desire to learn search logic, especially since most search logic reads like stereo instructions in another language. So to narrow your searches to manageable results you can do a mega search, using one of the mega search engines described below. These are starting to become more popular.

PROFUSION

Profusion (www.profusion.com) is a mega search engine, which means it performs your search simultaneously on other search engines. You can do your search at one central location and receive results back from other search engines. This service is free and easy to use. Rather than keying in your key word search on AltaVista and then doing the same search on Yahoo, you just go to Profusion and select the search engines you want to query, which saves you valuable time. This free service is continually improving its search results with new features and search capabilities. At last check, the search engines linked to this site were Yahoo, AltaVista, Excite, Magellan, InfoSeek, Lycos, Yahoo, Snap, WebCrawler, LookSmart, and GoTo.

FREE DOWNLOAD

If you are among those who are scared silly by the idea of searching resumes online or you don't want to be bothered with any part of search logic, you may want to try some automatic resume detectives. Nationjob has an online resume detective available, and you can download the software for free. (For more information or to download this free software, visit Nationjob at www.nationjob.com.) The program looks on major search engines for resumes matching your search criteria. All you need to provide is the job title, one or more skills, and location—city, state or province, and country.

USING SEARCH LOGIC

Warning! This section may contain computer-geek language and may not be suitable or appropriate for the average reader.

Another trick of the trade is knowing how to use the right key words to search. This is a very critical but fairly easy timesaving tool. All you need is a little guidance and practice. Almost every database seems to have its own little variance with search capabilities, but most work in a similar logical way when you use advanced search options or symbols. For example, Yahoo has several search options to help you narrow your search results. If you are getting resumes of engineering candidates in Japan and you only want those of computer programmers in Ohio, you are probably using the wrong search criteria. Advanced search techniques are available to you within Yahoo's search query box. Using the right syntax (combination of symbols and key words) will allow you to better tailor search results without having to visit the Search Options page. It also will allow you to tap into features currently not available through a regular search. There are four types of query syntax available.

1. *Required and Prohibited Search Words*: Attaching a plus sign (+) or a minus sign (-) will either require (+) or prohibit (-) words from appearing in the search results. "Systems Engineer+Unix" will turn up results with both "Systems Engineer" and "Unix" in

them. To prohibit a word from appearing in any of the search results, use the minus sign (-) in the exact same way.

2. *Document Section Restrictions*: Attaching one the following operators to the front of a search word will restrict the search to certain document sections. Attaching a "t:" will restrict searches to document titles only. Attaching a "u:" will restrict searches to document URLs. If you want titles you type: "t:recruiting," and for URLs you type "u:recruiting."

3. *Phrase Matching*: Putting quotes around a set of words will find results that match the words in that exact sequence. For example, "online recruiting" will find strings with those two words together. If you don't use quotation marks, some results will have just *online* in the text and others will have just *recruiting*.

4. *Wildcard Matching*: Attaching an asterisk (*) to the right-hand side of a word will return left-side partial matches. For example, "cap*" will find all matches with the letters *cap*.

   Combining the Syntax: You may combine any of the query syntax as long as it is combined in the proper order, which is the same order in which the operators appear on this page—that is, +, -, t:, u:, "", and lastly *.

If you take advantage of the push and the pull methods of sourcing resumes online, you will have enough resumes to keep you busy for quite a long time. Speaking of time, time is money and money is the bottom line. Don't be a victim of the "twilight zone phenomenon," which inexplicably happens to many people when they are online. They get lost and lose all track of time. They're not sure where all the time goes—it seems like they've been online for only a couple of minutes, and instead they look at the clock and discover that several hours have passed. Don't spend countless hours searching through resume data banks for candidates meeting job specifications. Remember that you also have some options of pulling resumes to you effortlessly. In Chapter 4, you will learn about more options available to help you find great candidates without having to perform even one search. These great tools will help you perfect the push method of recruiting online. They will also help you gradually wean yourself from the powerful addiction of searching resume banks. Instead, you will come to rely more on letting the computer do all the work. Hunting and pecking for resumes is not the most efficient way to recruit online, although many savvy recruiters are doing extremely well using this method.

Together We Stand, Divided We Fall

With the online information overload, I believe the future success of job banks will be through collaboration. Together we stand, divided we fall. Monster.com and Online Career Center (www.occ.com) joined together in January 1999 to provide maximum exposure for job seekers. In order to stay competitive, job sites will have to figure out a way to satisfy both customers—the job seekers and the staffing agencies of corporate employers. Servicing both clients presents quite a dilemma. Job seekers want the opportunity to submit their resume to one resume bank and have it automatically submitted to hundreds of other banks. Job banks want desperately to offer the best services to attract job seekers; however, the very thing they can do to benefit job seekers (distribute and make available their resumes to the widest possible audience) contradicts the job bank's goal of bringing in revenue from its staffing customers. At the time of this writing, there are already services offering this capability of multiple job postings. However, all the kinks haven't been completely worked out. Nevertheless, I predict more online job banks will build partnerships and conglomerates in order to serve both customers—job seekers and their client employers. Hopefully, in the near future the computer geniuses and innovative CEOs of the online world will figure out a way for both the job seeker and the HR professional to benefit.

KEY CONCEPTS

There are two ways you can accomplish the monumental task of sourcing resumes online. They are the pull method and the push method.

Play the game on the same playing fields as the job seeker. Use the same methods they use in their job search.

>> Look in the employment classified section of local newspapers or journals.

>> Network with friends, relatives, and colleagues.

>> Sign up with a recruiter, headhunter, or executive search firm.

>> Attend job fairs, canvass directly, and file applications with employers.

>> Mass mail unsolicited resumes with a broad marketing campaign.

Today, job seekers have these options plus many more. Some of the newer, more popular choices are

>> Attend a virtual job fair online (face-to-face interview via videoconference).

>> Create a virtual resume and post it to the web.

>> Apply online directly to employer's web site.

>> Search jobs on major, local, and niche recruiting sites and job posting boards.

>> Submit resumes to major, local, and niche recruiting sites with resume databases such as Hot Jobs, Monster.com, and so on.

>> Submit resumes to Usenet(s).

>> Submit resumes to select government agencies.

>> Submit resumes online to a trade organization or an online community.

>> Submit resumes to a career placement agency or an outplacement firm.

>> Sign up for automatic e-mail notification of jobs when employers post them.

>> Register with resume distribution services.

>> Directly canvass recruiters and employers by e-mail.

>> Register with a college-affiliated job bank.

>> Use a resume bureau search firm (which employers pay to search their resume base for candidates matching specific qualifications).

>> Register with a job site or resume bank confidentially.

Use search engines and mega search tools to speed up your search.

Seek out providers that are partnering and collaborating to offer the best services to both the job seeker and the recruiter.

Chapter Three
Recruitment Advertising

Recruitment advertising helps the job seeker find you and your web site. For job seekers, finding you can be difficult, so the trick to recruitment advertising is to help them find you painlessly and effortlessly. This chapter covers some leading companies' successful strategies for driving candidates to their front web door. One of the keys to successful online recruiting is to effectively market your web site. Remember the millions of job postings you have to compete with? Recruitment advertising won't nullify the competition, but if you follow the recommendations in this chapter, you will increase your success rate. Your targeted job seekers will be knocking at your web door before you know it.

As you may recall, recruitment advertising is the third component of online recruiting, after job postings and resume surfing. As mentioned in the previous chapters, job postings and resume surfing are primarily geared toward active job seekers. Recruitment advertising, however, targets both passive and active job seekers. You also need to keep in mind that the marketing strategy you decide to use should attract the types of candidates you are looking for. For example, if you are looking for engineers, you will probably have an entirely different recruitment advertising campaign than would someone recruiting sales professionals. You may recall the saying, "Birds of a feather flock together." To attract the flocks, you must advertise where they are migrating to on the web, such as an Engineering Society online bulletin board. Another way to tap into the vast numbers of people using the web—but not actively looking for employment—is to learn a few things about the typical Internet user. Knowing who's online, how long they are online, what they are doing when they're online, and where they're visiting online will help you direct your online advertising campaign appropriately.

Who's Online and What Are They Doing?

In the early days of the Internet, many nontechnical recruiters didn't want to bother with recruiting online because they felt the only people online were "techies." Well, times are changing, and the "techies" are becoming outnumbered by grandmothers and secretaries and high- powered executives.

What are these users doing online? Most Internet surveys show a breakdown like the one shown in the Fast Facts chart below.

FAST FACTS

Internet Usage

E-mail	82%
Local news/weather/sports	60%
Entertainment information	56%
Shopping information	42%
Education	40%
Financial investments	33%
Online banking	31%
Searching for employment	30%
Using auction sites	27%
Shopping for a car	22%

According to *Newsweek* (September 20, 1999), worldwide 225 million people can send and receive e-mail. Nationally, 46 percent of Americans send or receive e-mail every day and as many as 476 million instant messages are sent daily by AOL's 43 million registered users.

Shopping is another popular online activity, as is looking for employment. According to the American Internet User Survey from Cyberdialogue, 53 percent of current adult Internet users are male and 47 percent are female. For more information such as the above you can link to www.cyberdialogue.com. Founded in 1993, Cyberdialogue develops surveys covering such topics as business versus personal use, online commerce, trends, content preferences, and in-depth user demographics. With that many people using e-mail, you should at least consider the recruitment advertising possibilities of this method.

Advertise My Recruitment Opportunities via E-mail?

Junk mail and spam are everywhere. I almost hate to mention e-mail as a source for advertising because of all the spam already overflowing from our electronic mailboxes. However, since e-mail is one of the main uses of the Internet, it deserves mention here as a venue for recruitment advertising. Note that there is a difference between intrusive e-mail advertising and creative e-mail advertising. Spam is unsolicited mass e-mailing of junk advertisements similar to what we throw out on a daily basis from the regular postal service. Probably 99.9 percent of it is unwanted and totally annoying to the receiver. Some clever companies have found a creative way to be less intrusive while advertising their job postings via e-mail. Apart from job boards sending notices to job seekers and recruiters via e-mail, there are other ways to notify passive job seekers of opportunities. For example, if a newsletter goes to a particular industry via e-mail, you could easily put in a notice of your job opportunities at the closing of the newsletter. Some job seekers receive information on demand—such as stock quotes, weather, and news—via e-mail. Many providers, such as television and newspapers, offer advertisements for jobs to their "on-demand" e-mail customers. If you are targeting financial advisors, you should inquire about e-mail notifications going to financial brokers and their customers. You could advertise for a fee at the end of the stock price quotations or on your own company's e-mails. Think creatively and you will come up with some ideas to "push" your job opportunities to candidates in your particular industry.

Profile of a Passive Job Seeker

Since recruitment advertising also targets the passive job seeker, you should consider some key characteristics of the typical passive job seeker. Chart 5 provides a pretty good profile of passive job seekers. They may think about changing jobs from time to time when their current job gets a little too annoying, but for the most part they are not aggressively pursuing a job. So it is up to you to intrigue the job seeker enough to make the

CHART 5	PASSIVE JOB SEEKER PROFILE

Likes security

Workaholic

Dedicated

Hardworking

Information hound—likes to keep up to date on profession

Loyal employee (but willing to jump ship if not treated properly)

Open to entertaining attractive offers from time to time

Occasionally looks in the want ads or trade journals for positions of interest

Occasionally performs an online job search

Prefers to sign up for automatic job notifications via e-mail

Prefers to remain anonymous—confidentiality is critical

For the most part, is mildly happy and content in current job

Uses the Internet for information regarding work, professional development, and personal interests

first move. Interim Personnel and Monster.com have been doing a good job with their marketing campaigns targeting passive job seekers with tag lines such as "there is a better job out there." Interim's ad showed herds of sheep following each other aimlessly, with a loud, clear message—"get out of the herd and join Interim for a career."

Maximum Exposure Overdrive

Maximum exposure is the key word here. By splattering your web address and providing links all over popular web sites (especially where active and passive job seekers hang out), you will attract more people of higher caliber to your site. Many companies invest heavily in creating a professional web presence with beautiful graphics, video, sound—you name it. They hire the best web designers to make their site sing and dance. But so what if ABC Company spent $150,000 or more on its web site if very few people (customers and job seekers) come to visit it? If you have a web site, take this quick little test. Log onto the Internet and do a search for your company name on Yahoo, AltaVista, or any search engine. Does your company come up in the search engine? If not, try searching for a key word representing your line of business. Does your company come up in the first two or three pages of search results? If the answer is still no, let's try another test. Key in the words *engineering jobs* or *computer jobs* or whatever type of jobs you're recruiting for. If your company name doesn't come up in this search either, how do you think job seekers are going to find your job site? If you're with a well-known company you may have better luck; however, if you're with a small business, most job seekers will have never heard of you. (Most businesses can be classified as small—small businesses account for the majority of jobs.) So how do you get them to hear about your job openings? Following are the three main methods companies are using to drive job seekers to their recruitment site.

1. Increase the number of quality links to your site
2. Tap into the power of portals and high-traffic sites
3. Use a combination approach: advertise online and offline

Increase the Number of Quality Links to Your Site

One of the most critical factors defining online success for any web site is to have many quality links to other web sites. Links are interconnections all over the web connecting visitors on other sites to your site. The people at Marriott Hotel really know how to use links effectively in their online advertising. They have over 1,000 links to their web site from various places on the web. Just about every place online where you can register for travel, Marriott has a link. Viewers can zap right over to Marriott's web site where they can take your reservation. Later in this chapter you will learn where many people log onto the web. You should consider having many links and banners on popular financial, stock, and news pages to drive people to your site. Many private and nonprofit organizations will allow a free link to your site if you provide some value-added information to their customers or employees. It is common for a popular recruitment site to place links at over a thousand other web sites. Quality of links is especially critical since you can receive a better response from just two links on highly visited sites than from many links on low-traffic sites.

To determine how many links a particular site has is really quite simple. Many search engines on the Internet allow you to search for web sites that have links to other sites by selecting "search the web for links to this URL." You can simply type in the name of a site (for example, www.careermosaic.com) and quickly find out how many links it has. Links used to be free, but since they represent potentially high revenue, expect to pay some pretty hefty fees if you want a link on a major commercial site or portal (in other words, a high-traffic site).

Tap into the Power of Portals and High-Traffic Sites

The Fast Facts chart below shows an excerpt from the online Nielsen NetRatings. As you can see, the average time spent online is thirty minutes, with an average of four sites visited. Four sites on average! You need to think about how you can increase your chances of being seen from just four sites visited by the average user. One is more than likely a portal site.

A portal is an initial entry point such as America Online or Yahoo that most Internet users visit on a daily basis. Savvy online entrepreneurs generate traffic flow by advertising on these initial points of entry. I'm going to say it again to make my point clear—if you build it, they will not come if they don't have the road signs to find you. The road sign directing traffic to your site is your marketing campaign. Purchasing banner advertisements on popular, high-traffic sites such as America Online and CareerMosaic works extremely well. These web billboards help you build name recognition and drive passive and

FAST FACTS

Average time spent online per person: 30 minutes

4 sites visited per person

Total home Internet usage for the U.S.: 9.6 million hours online

Source: Nielsen NetRatings, December 26, 1999

active job seekers to your web door. By purchasing advertising on portals you are tapping into the advertising dollars already spent by the portal. When you advertise here you reap some of the return on their investment. Warning: There is a direct correlation between the cost of advertising and the traffic on these sites. Generally, the higher the traffic, the higher the price tag for you to advertise.

If you don't advertise and have links on a commercial site, you may be cheating yourself out of tapping into all this recruitment advertising spending—26 million dollars in 1998 by Monster.com alone! Most people have heard of Monster.com because of its massive online and offline marketing—even if they're not interested in changing jobs or finding employment. Monster.com is just one example of the hundreds of well-known recruitment sites spending millions of dollars to generate traffic to their site. Note: Forrester Research anticipates that by 2003, employers' online recruitment spending will reach $1.7 billion dollars.

Combination Approach

Using a combination approach—online and offline marketing—will also increase your exposure. As you can see in Chart 6, you have a variety of online and offline options to drive both active and passive job seekers to you.

CHART 6	OLD AND NEW MARKETING OPTIONS
Traditional Marketing Options	New Online Marketing Options
Print media: Newspapers, trade journals, magazines; direct mail campaign	Online advertisements: Banner/button advertisements on portals; banner/button advertisements on major job sites; banner exchange services
Word of mouth	Online links
Radio	E-mail
Television	

FAST FACTS

Portals Generating Referrals of Online Purchases

America Online 7.6%
Yahoo 4.1%
Netscape 3%
Excite 2.4%
AltaVista 2.2%
MSN 1.3%

*Source: Nua Internet Surveys,
June 24, 1999*

With the ease of Internet access, many people are going online to find information, though some are still using the traditional methods of watching television, reading newspapers, and listening to the radio. Many online marketers forget that these traditional methods should be used in combination with online advertising. Many companies are using a wide variety of online and offline marketing—radio, television, online advertising, and just about everything in between—to create brand awareness. A survey in February and March of 1999 by BizRate.com (survey base of over 1 million online buyers) found the results shown in this Fast Facts chart in terms of major portal sites as referrals for online business.

FAST FACTS

Offline Sources of Online Purchases

Print media 14%
Word of mouth 7%
Television 2%
Radio 1%
Other sources 9%
Total......... 33% of online
referrals came from
offline sources

Although major portals account for some purchase referrals, offline sources account for 33 percent of the referrals. Therefore, you need to look at both offline and online sources to maximize your recruitment advertising dollars. Even though your targeted job seekers may not necessarily be purchasers, this comparison shows the power of marketing. Marketing your web site has similar characteristics to marketing a product. So remember to use the approach successful companies are using—a combination of online and offline resources. This Fast Facts chart shows a breakdown of online referrals from offline sources.

Banner Exchange Services

Another popular advertising method is exchanging banner displays. You display banners for members of a network, and they in turn display banners for you. A portion of banner space is sold to sponsors, through whose support the network stays free of charge. There are hundreds of banner exchange services to choose from. One that has been around for a while is Link-Exchange, which provides a free fast counter you can download on your site if you want to keep track of how many visitors are clicking on your web site. For more information you can visit www.linkexchange.com.

Leading Companies and Their Strategies

Let's look at one of the pioneers in online recruiting. Cisco Systems is a $10-billion-a-year networking company. It hires 66 percent of its people and receives 81 percent of its resumes via the Internet (Useem, 1999). Cisco has even thought of a creative feature called the "Oh No! My Boss Is Coming!" button, which when clicked produces a screen titled "Seven Habits of a Successful Employee." This button is built into Cisco's employment web site in the event job seekers are searching for jobs while at work—they don't have to worry about getting caught looking for a better career. Pretty innovative, huh? No wonder Cisco can recruit 66 percent of its people using this method. I'll bet most of Cisco's new recruits are zapped from warm, comfortable seats in some very good companies—passive job seekers. Cisco, realizing that most passive job seekers probably don't have a current resume available, provides a simple, humorous Profiler to help potential candidates build a resume online.

Cisco Systems also invites information technology people to join a friend's community network. After a candidate registers, a Cisco employee in a position similar to the job seeker's potential position calls him or her to talk about the benefits of working at Cisco. Cisco has taken a digital nonpersonal method of online recruiting and transformed it into a personal one-on-one mentoring method. Kudos to Cisco Systems. The most impressive statistic regarding Cisco is its cost per hire—$6,556 versus an

---

FAST FACTS

>> Cisco Systems hires 66% of its people and receives 88% of its resumes via the Internet
Source: Fortune.com, "For Sale Online: You," Part 3, Jerry Useem, July 5, 1999

>> 90% of Cisco's early-stage job prospects log in from their current employer
Source: Fortune.com, "For Sale Online: You," Part 3, Jerry Useem, July 5, 1999

>> 72% of people polled search for jobs on employment sites
62% search for jobs on companies' web sites
Source: Hireadigm, "Posting Jobs on the Internet: What Price Awareness?" June 1999, Vol. 1, p. 2

---

industry average of $10,800. Additionally, the number of in-house recruiters has remained at around 100 even though the number of hires has risen from 2,000 to 8,000 people. What's more, Cisco has been able to fill an opening in about 45 days—down from 113 days in 1996 (Useem, 1999).

Another example of some innovative online recruiting is a website at Inacom, a 12,000-employee computer services firm in Omaha. This site features a game called TechnoChallenge. The game has flashy graphics combined with a series of technical questions. Contestants enter their name, professional information, and contact information to qualify for a drawing for a monetary prize. While contestants are having their technical aptitude tested, they don't realize they are also being screened by a technical recruiter. Those scoring high are contacted regarding potential employment.

Technisource is doing an excellent job of driving people to its site by advertising on a major job board. In June of 1999, Technisource had a large advertising banner spread across Monster.com's main home page. When you click on Technisource's banner you automatically get zapped over to its employment page of over 2,000 career opportunities.

The Flycatcher Approach

Our economy is enjoying full employment, and the competition to attract and hold the attention of in-demand candidates is fierce. Remember the "flycatcher approach"? You need sticky content in order to catch job seekers. The better the content, the more likely you are to get them to stick with your site. Content is a driving factor in attracting candidates. Keeping content up to date is also critical. You want loyalty, and a successful site will make users say to themselves, "Wow, I want to be able to remember this site, so I'd better bookmark it." Most Internet windows have some drop-down option for saving web address sites for easy future reference. For example, Microsoft Internet Explorer has an option on its top menu bar called "Favorites" where you can bookmark favorite sites in a file to retrieve any time you are online.

Successful sites are those that offer both unique value and rich content to job seekers and many timesaving services to recruiting professionals. We not only want it all but we want it at our fingertips. Job seekers want valuable content, useful information, and easy application or resume submission. Some want promotional articles to read, while others want to know which high-tech start-up companies are hiring. Some want to know how to negotiate a salary offer or a flexible working schedule. I believe the people operating most of the major job boards realize this. Some do a great job of servicing job seekers and others do a better job of servicing their customer accounts. Recruiters want to find candidates quickly and efficiently with the most user-friendly tools and technology available at a cost-effective price. There must be a balance between satisfying job seekers and satisfying recruiters, but job seekers should be the first priority. Still, CEOs of the web job world should continue to seek out better ways to service both customers.

KEY CONCEPTS

The key to successful online recruiting is effectively marketing your web site.

The two top ways to drive traffic to your site are

1. Increase the number of quality links to your site.

2. Tap into the power of portals and high-traffic sites.

Use the combination approach: advertise online and offline.

Ask yourself these ten questions to determine whether your recruitment site is effective:

1. Does your site target passive as well as active job seekers?

2. Is your site easy to navigate without a lot of slow-moving graphics?

3. Do you have advanced search capabilities to help job seekers narrow their search to only applicable jobs and locations?

4. Do you offer an option of talking to a live person for more information?

5. Does your recruitment site use the flycatcher approach, offering interesting, creative content for the job seekers you are recruiting?

6. Does your site offer interactive information such as contests, prizes, and giveaways?

7. Does your site offer an option for a confidential application process so the job seeker can make first contact anonymously?

8. Do you have an option to apply online with or without a resume?

9. Do you have a number of links on popular portals and commercial sites, or banner advertisements to drive traffic to your site?

10. Are job postings up to date and is content information accurate, with various options for job seekers to contact recruiters?

Be creative with the content of your site and follow leaders in their innovative recruiting methods.

Chapter Four

Tools and Tricks
That Make It Quick

This chapter includes all the tools and tricks—software and technology—that make recruiting online quick and painless. These tools will help you stay up to date on current online recruiting news, trends, and technology to help you increase your success. This chapter will also show you the sit-back-and-wait approach to recruiting. The power of technology is here to stay and we need to take advantage of some of these automatic agents to help us find job seekers to fill our critical job openings. Job seekers are using these tools and we need to be joining them so we can hook up and have a match made in online heaven. Following is a list of the top ten tools and tricks discussed in this chapter.

1. Stay current
2. Let the software do the work—the sit-back-and-wait approach
3. Shop around
4. Get statistics
5. Throw out the old rules of recruiting
6. Manage the scarcity
7. Seek out diversity
8. Manage the results
9. Outsource
10. Avoid the bug

Stay Current

Online recruiting newsletters are a great resource to help you stay up-to-date on the latest recruiting trends. As I have mentioned before, online recruiting is continually changing, and this fantastic medium is one way to keep abreast of all the changes in the online world. If you don't like receiving this type of information in e-mail format, you can read through online articles at the sites mentioned below instead.

ONLINE RECRUITING NEWSLETTERS

A popular newsletter that offers comprehensive online recruitment information is *Electronic Recruiting News* (ERN), edited by John Sumser. You can find this free newsletter at www.interbiznet.com. Interbiznet not only publishes daily newsletters, but also indexes previous newsletters and publishes a yearly Electronic Recruiting Index and Executive Summary. In addition, it delivers seminars all over the country on the topic of recruiting online. You can learn about new sites, job board rankings, recruiting tips, and more in the archives or newsletters.

Recruiting on the Web is an electronic newsletter published by Recruiter's Network, the Association for Internet Recruiting. It is free for HR professionals and recruiters. Recruiter's Network also offers a free resource center. Visit it at www.recruitersnetwork.com. The Network currently boasts a growth rate of fifty to a hundred new members a day. This newsletter provides statistics on who's online, new recruiting tools, seminar and training announcements, and more.

Best Recruiter News is another online newsletter devoted to the online HR professional. Published by the staff of Best Recruiter, it is located online at www.bestrecruit.com. At this web site, you can try out the current newsletter, participate in discussion groups with other recruiters, read back issues of the newsletter, and take advantage of all the other services Best Recruiter has to offer.

ONLINE DIRECTORIES

As you know by now, there are thousands of job sites available, with new ones popping up every day. To stay current with a comprehensive list of the thousands of existing and new job sites, you can visit two direc-tories, Job Hunt Guide at www.job-hunt.org and Riley Guide at www.dbm.com/jobguide.

Another great tool you can use to keep up to date is *CareerXRoads* (1998) by Gerry Crispin and Mark Mehler. This book is a directory of the best job, resume, and career management sites on the web. Frequent updates are available when you register via e-mail.

Let the Software Do the Work— the Sit-Back-and-Wait Approach

When we contemplate the tons of information (including resumes) available online, we soon realize we need help managing the informa-tion overload. First, we have to travel at light speed to get to what we want before someone else does, and then we have to filter out all the incomprehensible information blocking our view. Just as NASA uses probes and other advanced technology to explore the vast territories of outer space, we need tools to explore the Internet. You could spend every waking moment of the next twenty years searching through all the resumes online and not read them all. At last check America's Job Bank had over 400,000 resumes in its resume bank. That is why automatic matching technology has been invented, so you don't have to spend the rest of your life searching through all these resumes.

SPIDERS AND SNAKES AND BEARS—OH, MY!

I have arachnophobia and absolutely despise spiders—except for the ones that crawl around the web helping me with recruiting. These spe-cial spiders do what you tell them to do and weave their webs all night long while you are fast asleep. Spiders are sometimes referred to as snakes, robots, moles, rovers, and similar names. You can expect an explosion of spidering services in the near future. Services such as It-ta's Resume Robot (located at www.it-ta.com) are pioneering the field. These automated agents scavenge the web for new resumes that meet your criteria and send you the results in database format. This gives you and your company first shot at candidates as they enter their resumes online. The robot also can deliver a customized e-mail letter to prospective candidates. This service is not free (sorry to disappoint you) and at last check cost around $500 a month. For more information you can visit It-ta online.

Roverbot at www.roverbot.com will deliver your targeted e-mail addresses for about ten cents apiece. This is useful for targeting a specific group such as college students, specific alumni, or industry professionals. You tell the service the web address, and it roves around collecting e-mail addresses for you. WebSnake is a similar service that gathers e-mail addresses for you on your own desktop. Anaserve (www.anaserve.com) allows you to purchase robot software called "WebSnake." Once you buy it, it's yours forever without any other fees. A trial version and tutorial are available at www.homeuniverse.com/web.snake.htm.

My only caution to you in regard to any type of automatic e-mail distribution service is to make sure you are in compliance with all applicable laws, which change frequently. To avoid being accused of unwanted and illegal e-mail solicitation (spam), you must provide an option for people to remove their name from your distribution list. If you are not careful, you may run the risk of having your Internet account suspended. As handy as these tools may be, I prefer to send out my own individual messages to make first contact with a candidate. It takes longer, but I feel the personal approach makes a great first impression and results in a higher success rate. This is a decision you must make on your own, determined by your individual circumstances. If you have thousands of open requisitions to fill this year, my method may not be practical. If you do have quite a few requisitions to fill, you can use shell documents with e-mail the same way as you can with online job postings. For example, you can save a standard greeting and introduction about your company in one of your e-mail folders and reuse it. You provide job seekers with detailed information on your jobs and company in your shell e-mail. All you have to remember is to type in individual names to personalize the message.

Personic Resume Agent (located at www.ezaccess.com), formerly known as Robosurfer, is a full-featured Internet agent that locates and retrieves resumes from personal home pages or relevant resume newsgroups on the Internet. Personic Resume Agent communicates with ten major Internet search engines and makes search requests like a human does, but faster and more comprehensively. It merges required skills and geographic criteria with multiple search phrases often found in resumes and then searches several Internet search engines simultaneously. Personic Resume Agent then connects to the URLs returned by the search engines and processes each web page to determine whether it matches the criteria. Each resume that matches the criteria is passed directly into a searchable back-end database with the e-mail address, street address, city, state, zip, telephone, fax, URL, page title, and skills set. The resumes are then placed into separate databases. Duplicates are eliminated via a merge-and-purge option, saving the time and effort of reviewing the same resume multiple times. Resumes can then be viewed and sorted to narrow the pool of candidates.

Most resume robots, spiders, snakes, and so on have similar software features. They all strive to reduce the amount of time you spend on the web searching for quality resumes and/or e-mail addresses. Almost all of them allow you to search according to your specific search criteria. The differences among them lie primarily in their respective software menus and ease of use of the software. They can also differ in the types of data they retrieve. Some retrieve only e-mail addresses and URL web addresses, while others target resumes or resume banks. For instance, infoGIST.com is a site that allows you to search leading resume banks. Using infoGIST.com software, you can reduce your search time by 90 percent. InfoGIST.com offers two packages for recruiters. The first package, Resume infoFinder, lets you instantly and simultaneously search top resume sources. The other package, Resume infoFinder Gold, allows you to search fee-based resume sites and resumes on your computer or intranet. More information and free fourteen-day trial software can be found online at www.infogist.com.

JUNGLEE TECHNOLOGY

With all these critters crawling around, it's no wonder we have something called Junglee (www.junglee.com) to tame the jungle. Junglee provides the middleware to move jobs or information from your site to targeted databases. While the front end of the web is well known and familiar, the "back end" is changing rapidly. Junglee's technology is an approach to making complex data work together. The flexibility of this technology will be key to continued growth of online recruitment. Junglee has been touted for its ability to turn a jungle of web sites into a superstore so users can comparison shop online.

The trend I see for Internet recruiting is this type of back-end service, which is transparent to the user but operates behind the scenes to link things smoothly. For example, smaller job sites interconnect in the background to well-known career hubs. A technical scientist might be on www.sciencejobs.com and see a job she's interested in. When she clicks on the job for more information, she's transported to another site through what is called a multiple point of entry. She may not realize she's at a larger site surrounded by other job postings she may not be interested in. I don't agree with this marketing strategy because it seems a bit deceptive to job seekers. It seems to take value away from niche sites, which are niches because they attract a specific audience. But I have faith that technology will probably take care of this little problem by offering some advanced type of targeted search query to specific disciplines or categories.

Junglee's CEO is Rakesh Mathur. He is doing everything he can to draw attention to Junglee, and he's doing a good job. He already has the attention of these major players: AOL Digital Cities, CareerCity, *Boston Globe*, CareerMosaic, CareerPath, *Chicago Tribune*, Classifieds2000, CareerMagazine, *Wall Street Journal*, Westech Virtual Job Fair, *Washington Post*, and *San Jose Mercury News*.

CROSS-POSTING SERVICES

As promised in Chapter 1, here are some cross-posting services. To refresh your memory, cross posting allows you to post to multiple sites (from your web site or another host site) with only one data entry. There is a monthly or per-posting fee. These services provide maximum exposure on leading sites while saving you keystrokes and data entry time. Some services partner with major sites such as Yahoo or Headhunter and others partner with more local or niche sites.

There are several methods of delivery for these services—software download, CD, or web address with a password. Methods of inputting information and maintaining (updating or deleting) your job orders may differ. I personally wouldn't choose a site that doesn't allow for immediate updates to my job orders. If I fill a requisition on a Monday, for example, I want to have the job order deleted that same day or at the very latest the next day. Some sites have a "once your job order is gone, it's gone" policy. You can't retrieve it, modify it, or delete it until the allotted time frame has expired. Unless you want to hear from job seekers long after your job order is filled, I wouldn't patronize any service not offering flexibility in modifying your jobs after they're entered. Even though these nonflexible services usually offer a lower cost, the time you save with services that offer modification flexibility may make them more economical. I also recommend you try out as many free trials and free memberships as are available. Experiment with the many different systems and software packages out there until you've found one that meets all your needs and that you feel the most comfortable using. Most reputable cross-posting services will allow you to try before you buy. You can determine for yourself whether it is user-friendly and provides the tracking ability and level of service you want packaged with this service. Some work better for nationwide companies, while others may be better for smaller operations. You have many cross-posting providers to choose from, some of which are described below.

GO Jobs

GO Jobs (www.gojobs.com), based in southern California, was founded in 1996 as an online job board. It has partnered with most major job boards on the Internet to create the GO Jobs Recruiting NETwork™, an electronic job distribution system. You can enter jobs once, then GO Jobs electronically manages them on most major job boards. For example, let's say you currently have a membership on Dice and you also post to Headhunter and Yahoo Classifieds for maximum exposure. Rather than manually entering the jobs on three different job sites, GO Jobs provides the software for you to enter the job once and then automatically adds your job postings to Dice, Headhunter, Yahoo, and related newsgroups. Changing, deleting, and adding new jobs on multiple sites is easy. GO Jobs offers free software and a thirty-day trial period. Thereafter, if you decide to sign up for membership, you can expect to pay around $400 a month for unlimited job postings uploaded to America's Job Bank, Yahoo, and Headhunter.

SelectJobs

SelectJobs is a cross-posting service I stumbled across through America's Job Bank, the free government-sponsored site available through the U.S. Department of Labor. One day I was searching through America's Job Bank and I noticed a job posting that read "This job was posted by SelectJobs." So, of course, I had to find out what SelectJobs was all about. This is a terrific service that cross posts your job openings to some highly exposed sites such as America's Job Bank and Yahoo.

Founded in 1996, SelectJobs targets the information technology and high-tech fields. This site advertises in computer magazines and trade journals targeting these candidates. This is a must for the IT recruiter and companies looking for computer professionals—and just about everyone has this type of opening to fill. CareerShop also offers a matching service agent ensuring the best matches between candidates and employers. You're probably thinking, this sounds so good, it will probably cost me a small fortune. Well, in my opinion, this service is well within most folks' budget. The membership cost as of December 1999 was $350 per month for up to 250 job postings. Membership includes resume matching and resume search, as well as cross posting to the following popular web sites and over 400 newsgroups: AltaVista, America's Job Bank, Classifieds2000, Classifieds Warehouse, ERPCentral.com, JVsearch.com, ORAsearch.com, ProHire.com, unixADMINsearch.com, Vault.com, VBOnline.com, and Yahoo. For an additional fee, SelectJobs can also customize your cross posting to increase your visibility significantly by including these high-traffic employment sites: Career Magazine, JobOptions, Monster.com, and Nationjob.

Some of these sites are free, such as America's Job Bank, Yahoo, and newsgroups. There is a fee for Classifieds2000, so you have to decide for yourself whether the additional exposure is worth $350. Your other options are to manually post your jobs yourself, to purchase software such as Net Recruiter (discussed in the following paragraph), or to assign one of your internal computer geniuses to write a program to automatically cross post jobs for you.

Note that as of January 2000 SelectJobs merged with CareerShop. The combined company will go by the name of CareerShop. All services and posting sites mentioned here will be carried over.

Net Recruiter

There are quite a few choices for cross-posting services. Some charge by the level of usage, so cost-effectiveness depends on whether you post ten or ten thousand jobs. I have tried to give enough information on a wide variety of services so that you can make informed decisions. If you are really brave and savvy, you may want to try purchasing cross-posting software and doing this yourself. Net Recruiter provides the software for around $100 as well as a free thirty-day trial. Net Recruiter has been receiving some wonderful kudos and although the menus take some getting used to, with minimal training you can impress even your computer guru co-workers. You can find out more about this software at www.joblocator.com. At this site, the Internet Job Locator, you can also choose other cool tools such as automatic e-mail searches. You request the type of resumes you are searching for by key words, and every morning Job Locator sends you electronic resumes that matched your search criteria. Each search returns the first fifty resumes that most closely matched your key words. There is a fee structure for this service that is determined after you set up your account and decide what level of service you want. For example, for each job credit you can post one job and for each resume credit you receive an automatic e-mail resume search for 21 days. After that you may sign up for more job credits. Resume credits may be reused throughout the duration of the membership and are renewed monthly. At the end of the month, resume credits are issued back to your account.

CareerShop

CareerShop (www.careershop.com) is dedicated to making online recruiting easy. It is a cross-posting service that is very similar to SelectJobs. This similarity may be the reason these two popular sites decided to merge and operate as one site as of January 2000. All sites SelectJobs posted to will be continued and posted by CareerShop. The combined site will be known as CareerShop.

CareerShop has access to several premium resume databases, and for a fee of $350 (as of July 1999 and subject to change) you can have one of its team members search for you. Within three business days you will receive a FedEx package of from ten to thirty hard-copy resumes best matching your job order(s). CareerShop also offers some other timesaving strategies such as unlimited job postings, automatic notification of resumes matching your job requirements, and cross-posting services. It will distribute (cross post) your jobs to other major job sites, newsgroups, and popular sites such as Yahoo and Classifieds2000. You can get a picture of the magnitude of reach offered by CareerShop by visiting its web site.

All In One Submit

All In One Submit is another cross-posting service with some big clients, such as Keane, Technisource, Kelly Technical, Computemp, Motorola, Xerox, EDS, Holiday Inn, General Employment, McDonnell Douglass, and Humana. These companies and others have signed up to target computer professionals and in-demand candidates. All In One Submit cross posts to multiple job sites such as America's Job Bank, Yahoo, and Headhunter for one low monthly fee. You select the sites you want to post to. This is a little different from SelectJobs, where your jobs are automatically sent to the partner sites. With All in One Submit you have a little more control (if that's what you like) over where your jobs are posted to. Some of the choices are Yahoo, Headhunter, America's Job Bank, Jobs Online, America Online job newsgroups, Netshare, CareerMarketplace, MedBulletin, and specific Usenet job newsgroups. To find out more and to sign up, visit its web site at www.allinonesubmit.com.

Careerspan

Careerspan (www.careerspan.com) is a fairly new cross-posting site targeting high-tech professionals. There's a wide range of information at this site. It has online job fairs, hotlinks to your corporate home page, banner advertising, virtual resumes, and, of course, cross-posting services. It currently cross posts to Yahoo, Deja News, and AltaVista, with additional sites coming on board in the near future. It has yearly and monthly memberships and different price packages starting below $100 a month for unlimited postings. Careerspan, in my opinion, is doing a pretty good job in the area of offering content-rich information to the hard-to-reach high-tech professionals.

Job Net

Job Net, located at www.jobnet.com, specializes in packaging some of the best job databases for employers on the Internet and helps them manage the results. Some of the partnerships they have formed are with 4Work, America's Job Bank, Career Magazine, CareerSite, CareerWeb, Job Options, Headhunter, JobWeb, Nationjob, Job Net, and Yahoo. Job Net offers resume management services by e-mail, fax, or mail.

Computerwork

Computerwork (www.computerwork.com) is a fairly new premier site for matching computer job seekers and their skills to requirements of the nation's best recruiting firms. Programmers, database administrators (DBAs), analysts, network engineers, and all IT/IS professionals can search its substantial job board for over 10,000 computer jobs in areas such as COBOL, C++, Java, Powerbuilder, Oracle, SAS, and others. Job seekers post their resumes, which are matched with profiles of member companies. Some of Computerwork's key features are distributing resumes via e-mail, cross posting to other popular job sites (such as Yahoo, Headhunter, and America's Job Bank), unlimited job postings for one fee, and unlimited access to its resume bank.

COMPUTER-ASSISTED INTERVIEWS

Major manufacturing companies, accounting firms, and companies in the retail business are starting to turn to computer-assisted interviewing to conduct first rounds of interviews—without any human resources involvement. This method allows busy human resources staff to quickly screen out inappropriate and unqualified applicants. Automated phone systems such as Reid Systems® have been around for several years. In these systems, the computer's phone technology screens candidates for jobs by asking specific job-related questions. The candidates answer by pressing buttons on the telephone. If they answer inappropriately, the screening session ends and the candidates are not considered further.

The next step in automated interviewing tools is interactive online systems working off corporate web sites. These interactive systems offer internal tracking and forwarding capabilities to bring job seekers to your web site, where they answer some online questions by completing a profile—then the system manages the results. This area is likely to grow because everyone is heading to web sites to build companies' products and images, get information, and attract candidates. It just makes sense to provide online interactive interviewing systems. One company offering this is Employ America (www.employamerica.com). You can find out more about their services or receive a free demo by contacting them at 1-800-807-9675.

ONLINE VIDEO INTERVIEWING

Career Magazine (www.careermag.com) is a pioneer in offering video interviewing (where you can interview face to face via computer video technology). Its SearchLinc interview studios networked around the United States feature state-of-the-art videoconferencing hardware and software. In addition, employers and colleges are hosting increasing numbers of virtual job fairs, where recruiters can video interview candidates anywhere in the country.

By offering video interviewing you shorten the recruiting cycle and save money—no travel costs, reduction in non-value-added recruiting expenses, and more real-time face-to-face interviews in a shorter time period. A company can video interview ten candidates and select only three out of the ten to fly to the company for an in-person interview with other levels of management or to present a job offer.

Shop Around

Fraud is everywhere! According to Internet Fraud Watch, operated by the National Consumers League, complaints have increased 600 percent since 1997. Online auctions were the number one fraud complaint in 1998. More people are online and more people are getting scammed. One of the top ten scams, according to Internet Fraud Watch, is home-based employment opportunities. You need to make sure the sites you use have fraud patrol so that your potential employees are not getting scammed right next door to your employment advertisement.

When you are shopping for a new house or a new car, the best advice is to shop around and do business with someone you trust. The same holds true in the online recruiting business. Most of the sites mentioned in this book have been around for some time and for the most part are not fly-by-night or scam operations. However, the best advice I can give you is to shop around and see if you can get some referrals and recommendations. If a job seeker or other recruiter has had some awful experience with a site, you can expect a similar experience. Some of the sites mentioned in this book or elsewhere may not be suitable for your business. You need to shop around and know whom you're doing business with. Ask other professionals, listen to what the media in your area are saying, and ask the job seekers. Also ask them where they heard about your job opportunities. Find out what's working in your geographic area. You may find that a local niche site or a combination of a few sites is required to reach the areas you're recruiting in.

Get Statistics

Another method you can use to determine who's the best is to stay up to date on the latest statistics on online sites. You can receive up-to-date statistics on employment sites and other online information at Hitbox (www.hitbox.com). Hitbox says it is not associated with any existing web site and that it will remain completely unbiased. It wants to provide the quickest and most accurate statistics on the Internet with fair ranking to all joining members. On July 9, 1999, Dice was ranked first, with the highest number of visitors. If you don't like to rely on statistics alone, and you want more expert opinions on who's the best, read on.

COMPARE HIT RATES AND NUMBERS OF LINKS
Another important thing to know is the number of links a site has to other sites on the Internet. As we have discussed, links are critical to online success. The more links a site has (especially if the links are on high-traffic

sites), the more visitors it will receive. One of the leading search engines is Hotbot (www.hotbot.com), where you can ask how many links are in its database to the employment site. For example, you can type in www.careermag.com and in a few seconds the search engine will return the number of links this site has and list each site. Other search engines offer this tool as well. Just look for a drop-down box that reads "search the web for links" or "search links." To be considered a major employment site, the site should have a minimum of a couple thousand links to its site. Quality of links is also important. I would rather see fewer links to high-traffic hubs or portals than more links to sites I have never heard of.

Are the sites you are posting to (or cross posting to) linked to any other sites you would rather not have potential customers or candidates viewing? For example, if you are posting to ABC Job Board, which has a link to Home Based Opportunities, which lists only jobs resembling get-rich-quick schemes, job seekers are likely to be discouraged from visiting your site. As ever-increasing links and subdirectories within subdirectories are clouding the Internet, recruiters must make sure they know whom they are dealing with. As pay-per-link options (where high-traffic sites are selling links) are becoming more popular, I see this problem growing rather than shrinking.

One area I haven't mentioned so far is the influx of sex-related job sites. Some pornographic sites are getting more creative with their URL addresses to give the appearance of a business or employment site. An example is whitehouse.com. This site has nothing to do with any government issues. I make this point because a site that has the appearance of a job board may have a naked body or two lurking in the background. It would be very time consuming (if not impossible) to verify all the links to a job board, but one thing you can do is search on a search engine like Hotbot to see if anything unusual comes up in the site names listed in the links.

Throw out the Old Rules of Recruiting

Those who sit back and don't harness the power of the Internet will lose the battle to attract in-demand candidates. There are online and offline methods to help you learn this new way of recruiting. If you recruit for a large, well-known, profitable company, in the old days your difficulty would have been too many candidates to screen, with the number of resumes far exceeding the number of available openings. Now many recruiters in well-known companies are having difficulty filling their highly skilled positions. They are sometimes having more difficulty than the new start-up companies that use innovative recruiting methods. We must treat potential candidates like we treat potential customers—with the utmost respect, courtesy, and superior customer service. If you are not doing so, you're not playing by the new rules of recruiting.

PUT YOUR JOB SEEKER'S SHOES ON AND LEAVE THEM ON

Throwing out the old rules also means putting on your job seeker's shoes. What would attract you to the position you are trying to fill? What creative benefits and frivolous fringes do you need to offer job seekers you are recruiting? What is your competition doing? Are they offering sign-on bonuses, free training, or luxury cars? This is not a joke—some companies are offering expensive cars to employees as an enticement to join the company. Attitudes and hot candidates' desires differ sharply— from BMWs to flexible scheduling. Don't be afraid to ask new recruits which benefit attracted them most or the reason they accepted the job offer. You also need to ask the candidates refusing job offers what it would take for them to join the company.

You might even want to pretend you are a job seeker applying for the job. Call the staffing agency or the person responsible for filling your opening and determine for yourself whether you are welcomed or you feel like a door is slamming in your face. See if applying for a job you have posted is an easy task or a difficult one. You may never know what your clients experience unless you put on those job seeker's shoes and walk through recruiters' doors, web doors, job banks, and competitors' doors.

Manage the Scarcity

If you've never heard of just-in-time recruiting, then you are not managing the scarcity. Recognizing that labor shortages are reaching critical proportions, visionary companies such as Intel and Microsoft have begun developing long-term relationships with candidate pools. Intel has a successful relationship with San Jose State University, and Microsoft has one with the developer community. You may have a long-standing partnership with a university where you do on-site recruiting once or twice a year, but just-in-time recruiting takes this further. It requires anticipating future needs and future job openings at your company. Developing a critical pipeline of available candidates will be the key to successful recruiting in the future. Too often companies recruit heavily just prior to college graduations rather than on an ongoing basis. The theory is that labor supply can be managed like any other production ingredient—by establishing relationships early within school districts, college communities, professional organizations, and other targeted areas, you are managing the labor scarcity. Just five years ago job seekers networked for future positions. Now job seekers are finding jobs more frequently than ever before and being lured by the juiciest offers. Building a network of loyal candidates requires good recruiting know-how because of the labor outlook and low unemployment figures. As a new millennium recruiter, start thinking of ways to build your network through professional organizations, clubs, sports activities, colleges, and online communities.

Seek out Diversity

To be successful you must seek out diversity. Management recruiters will have to widen their market penetration and network with different online communities as well as the real world. No longer will recruiting at only the Ivy League colleges and establishing alliances with the "same old" networks work in the future. Clients will expect a more diverse range of candidates. They may even demand someone on your staff concentrating full-time efforts strictly on handling diversity recruiting. Visiting specific organizations online is an effective method of recruiting diverse job seekers in specific disciplines. Yahoo has a great directory of online organizations and groups. Its directory list includes a vast array of associations representing specific trade organizations and special interest groups. Under the heading Professional Associations, Yahoo has over 180 ranging from the very well known to the little known. Some examples include American Management Association, American Association of Hispanic Certified Public Accounts, American Society of Association Executives, Business and Professional Women, Association of Women Engineers, and National Black MBA Association.

Another professional society where you can find candidates on or off the Internet is the American Institute of Chemical Engineers and Certified Public Accounts. There are American societies of microbiology, mechanical engineers, civil engineers, ceramic engineers, quality engineers, and nondestructive testing engineers. There are institutes of electrical engineers, electronics engineers, and industrial engineers. Chances are, just about any discipline you are recruiting for can be found online with a click of the mouse.

Manage the Results

Following are some statistics on how Microsoft, Inc., is managing the influx of resumes.

Even though Bill Gates believes our success depends on how we gather, manage, and use information, many companies are not using resume

---

FAST FACTS

>> Microsoft, Inc., receives 600 to 900 resumes from job applicants every day, either by post mail or e-mail or online via Microsoft's web page Resume Builder (p. 41)

>> All resumes are electronically matched with open job positions within 24 to 48 hours of receipt (p. 41)

>> Microsoft hired 85 people per week during 1997 (p. 42)

>> "How you gather, manage, and use information will determine whether you win or lose" (p. 3)

Source: Bill Gates, Business at the Speed of Thought

management software. A survey conducted by the independent research firm McKendrick and Associates ("Classifieds Still the Way . . . ," 1999) on behalf of the William Olsten Center for Workforce Strategies found that only 16 percent of U.S. executives polled say their companies use resume management software. This leads me to believe that with all the resumes floating around the Internet, filed electronically, on managers' desks, in HR departments, and in the mail, one obstacle to filling our human resource requirements may be that we just can't find the right resumes at the right time.

Wouldn't you like to have a system you could rely on to do all the work for you? Wouldn't you love to be able to press a button and have a neat list of fully qualified candidates ready to interview for your hot job? Or to send to the hiring manager(s) to review in a matter of seconds versus months? Well, the good news is there are many sophisticated systems available for you to choose from. They can help you manage today's results as well as help you prepare for future job openings you're not even aware of yet.

RESUME TRACKING SYSTEMS DESIGNED TO SAVE YOU TIME

So if you're not familiar with resume tracking systems and software, you're probably wondering if there really is something that will extract, retrieve, compile, sort, and deliver a manageable short list of outstanding candidates. Well, the answer is yes and no. In a perfect world you can expect to review the premier list, but get real—this world is far from perfect. Even the snazziest software that you purchase by taking out a second mortgage on the business isn't perfect. Words only make sense to a computer when programmers tell it what to recognize and what to make sense of. For example, you can tell the computer to retrieve the words *Monty Python*, but the computer's intelligence will most likely associate the word python with snakes. The associations we take for granted are not easily programmed into the computer. So when your search results in someone on the short list you would never have considered because they've been working with snakes for the last ten years and you were looking for an actor versed in Monty Python, be forgiving. Great efforts are currently being made to eliminate this type of nuisance.

Restrac WebHire Network

Restrac and Resumix are both reputable leaders in the area of resume tracking. Restrac (www.restrac.com) designs, develops, markets, and supports the entire hiring process for more than ninety Fortune 500 companies. It is one of the leading providers of networked recruiting solutions, including resume scanning, applicant tracking, requisition management, and hiring. Restrac has been around since 1982, with revenues in the double-digit millions and continued growth anticipated. Restrac is a registered trademark of Restrac, Inc. WebHire and PartnerPools are service marks of Restrac, Inc. All other products and services mentioned may be trademarks or registered trademarks of their respective owners.

In November of 1998 Restrac introduced the WebHire Network. WebHire has partnered with other online job banks, which allows recruiters to use a standard web browser to post jobs, search and retrieve resumes, and access pre-employment services. The WebHire Network reduces some of the administrative tasks of managing multiple recruiting tasks through consolidation of activities. It has a client base of more than 375 companies worldwide. Among its customers are American Express, AT&T, Millennium Pharmaceuticals, and Microsoft. According to Tim McManus, Vice President of Internet products at Restrac, "Network is a natural evolution of the strengths and capabilities Restrac has relied on to meet the changing needs of the industry for the past seventeen years. Combining industry-leading automated recruiting solutions, Internet expertise, and strategic alliances with recruiting service providers, they've created a single Internet connection that provides a complete range of online recruiting capabilities for businesses of any size or industry." Also in November 1998, Restrac announced it had purchased the Junglee technology, which currently powers many leading Internet career sites including the Washington Post's CareerPost Classified job search site and the Wall Street Journal Interactive Edition's employment site. Restrac customers will have access to these networks by placing open positions on its corporate web site. WebHire starts at around $500 per month. The pricing structure includes full use of the WebHire software, posting access to multiple career sites, and searching Restrac pools of resumes.

Resumix

Resumix (www.resumix.com), offering resume database management tools, is a leader in the art of computerized interpretation of candidate resumes. At the core of its powerful system is Knowledge Base, which goes beyond simply matching key words and determines skills based on context. It matches skills to the position criteria. The Resumix people have a goal of perfecting the key word search to surpass the human knowledge base. They provide sophisticated candidate searches with more precise matching of personnel needs. They've also partnered with some major job posting sites to offer a powerful solution called Internet Recruiter, which allows you to post to hundreds of large, diverse Internet recruiting hubs. Some other features of the Internet Recruiter are the ability to prescreen applicants via an online questionnaire, productivity reports, and an online resource center. This is similar to the computer-assisted interview process discussed in the previous chapter. In the future, I hope to see more software and web sites offering this automated resume screening technology.

Some of the key features you receive from the Resumix Internet Recruiter are job postings to over 600 job sites, unlimited access to the internal resume database, ranked listing of all applicants scored against the requirements for the job, comprehensive reports on job posting effectiveness, and unlimited access to categorized HR information. Using Internet Recruiter's InternetPost™ function, you also have access to hundreds of job sites such as Monster.com, CareerMosaic, Job Options, Nationjob, and the many niche sites such as Developers Net Community (www.developers.net) and Accounting and Finance Jobs (www.accountingnet.com). You point and click to the mega sites, niche sites, and user groups of your choice. These choices are updated by the Internet Recruiter cyberstaff, who are on the watch for new trends in recruiting and new job sites on the net.

Resumix also offers a unique prescreening feature called ICES™. This cool tool acts as a filter for applicants based on their responses to a brief online questionnaire. You or a recruiter assign the weight of importance to each question. ICES then ranks and sorts the candidates. This reduces the number of unqualified candidates entering the Resumix database. Internet Recruiter also has a reporting feature, ReportSite, which helps you keep track of job postings and responses. You analyze the effectiveness of online job campaigns to determine which sites are working best for you. These reports allow recruiters to understand the return on investment from Internet job postings and responses.

Resumail Recruiter

Employers of all sizes (some government agencies, too) use Resumail Recruiter™ to post job openings that can only be applied for on the Internet. Awarded a five-star rating by ZDNet, a leading online magazine of Ziff-Davis Publishing Company, Resumail software offers job seekers immediate access to current jobs posted by employers as well as a way to create and submit resumes electronically. Resumail Recruiter 4.0 working in conjunction with Resumail Network and Resumail software ensures direct, confidential communication between job seekers and employers across the Internet.

Resumail Recruiter improves efficiency by allowing instant posting of jobs in a Windows® environment. It gives ample space to post your company's profile/benefits, a summary of current openings, and a detailed description of the jobs posted. Your web site on Resumail Network has a "Resumail It" hot button on every page. If there are no job openings posted, interested candidates can submit their resumes to your general folder on your profiles/benefits page to be considered when any job openings become available. With this button, you can also "Resumail enable" your web site so candidates can resumail their resumes directly. It also allows you to import resumes in the database program of your choice or print them in the format of your choice. For more information regarding this service, visit www.resumail.com.

HireSystems

HireSystems offers web-based hiring management, applicant tracking, and resume processing services. It has made the expensive infrastructure investment so you don't have to. HireSystems will take all the resumes you receive, in any format—paper, fax, e-mail, or online—and put them into a secure, private database. Anyone in your organization can search the resume database for the best candidates, forward them to the right people, and track the applicants through the hiring process. You can find out more about HireSystems online at www.hiresystems.com.

There you have it—a brief introduction to some very good service providers. I would like to suggest that you pay particular attention to current and future needs prior to investing in any resume maintenance service. Take a good look at your five-year plan (or envision what your company will look like in five years) to determine what capabilities are needed now and will be needed in the future. Do you expect to be growing at a fast rate and hiring quite a few employees over the next few years? Try to invest in a system that will grow with you or allow you to add services and features on an as-needed basis. Determine whether your current system is cost-effective or costing you money. How much time are valuable personnel spending on handling resumes that are of no interest to your company? What is the cost of having unfilled positions in your organization? What is the cost of having your valued customers not receiving the level of service you promised them due to empty critical positions? You have a wide variety of service providers and price ranges to choose from. When I typed in the key words *applicant tracking* on Yahoo's search engine, I found over 500 vendors quite capable of handling your needs. I encourage you to do a little research on your own to find out as much as you can about this software. You may even have resume-tracking software already built into your payroll, time, and attendance (or other) software and not be using it to its full advantage.

The organizations that can shorten the hiring cycle and simplify human resource functions will reap more advantages than just cost savings—they may be saving their business.

Outsource

Outsourcing has become a very popular option for many companies. Everything from recruiting new hires to training has been successfully performed outside of the company walls.

Even some aspects of the production process and routine paperwork are outsourced. You can save money and time and be more efficient when you hire specialized people who are in business to provide just the service you want to outsource. If someone else can do it better and more cost-effectively, shouldn't you consider it? Outsourcing payroll is a common practice now, but just twenty years ago many companies wouldn't even consider outsourcing such a critical aspect of their business. Whether yours is a large, small, or medium-sized company, you should seriously consider outsourcing some aspect of the recruiting process. Some outsourcing firms in the area of researching resumes are listed below.

ELECTRONIC RESEARCH BUREAUS

One available outsourcing option is electronic research bureaus (ERBs). You can take advantage of ERBs by merely picking up a phone. These services are a viable option when you are looking for critical skills in a specific industry and know the skill set will be very difficult to find and recruit. For example, a company in the thin film business may require a specialized set of skills in its engineers and process specialists. An ERB could help in penetrating another supplier or competitor to research any candidates who might be looking to transfer. This is a delicate situation and requires confidentiality in sourcing valuable employees with skills you need who are already working for someone else. The ERB might be located in California and you might be recruiting for New York—geography doesn't matter.

You would give the ERB your specifications, such as "I'm looking for a systems engineer with three to five years' work experience, a B.S. degree in computer science, a strong Unix proficiency, and Solaris background. A plus for the candidate would be computer industry experience working for a company such as Sun Microsystems." The researchers, for a fee, will provide you with a report and/or resumes of candidates meeting your criteria. Most electronic research bureaus provide some variation of the above service. Some offer a wider variety or more customized services to fit your individual circumstances. All search out candidates working at specific employers or in specific industries, looking in their own database, the Internet's vast supply of resumes, or a combination of these. They do the research while you just sit back and write a check for their service.

SkillSearch

One research bureau I've heard some good things about is SkillSearch, located at www.skillsearch.com. In business since 1990, it is rapidly becoming one of the leaders in alternative recruiting. SkillSearch usually has around 60,000 to 70,000 members in its database—99 percent have a four-year degree and 50 percent have an advanced degree. The average work experience of the job seekers in its database is eight years. SkillSearch researches and extracts details about each candidate by requiring each member to fill out an extensive questionnaire. This provides for better employer-candidate matchmaking. If you're not satisfied with the search results, SkillSearch will fine-tune your search until you are satisfied. It offers four recruiting services.

1. It recruits by member referrals and by partnering with over 140 alumni and professional associations and other major resume banks.
2. It also receives fresh recruits from its extensive mail marketing campaign, mailing monthly solicitations to over 500,000 potential job seekers.
3. The company provides a service it calls Recruiting Links, geared toward driving quality candidates to your job openings through banner advertisements. You receive traceable results in the form of a monthly report telling you the amount of traffic the site generated for your company.
4. One of the newest service options offered by SkillSearch is Employ-MAIL, which e-mails your job ads directly to targeted candidates. Job seekers fill out a brief profile identifying their occupation, education, language capabilities, location preference(s), and e-mail address. SkillSearch enters the candidates' information into the EmployMAIL database. You submit a profile identifying the target audience for your job. SkillSearch then e-mails your job posting directly to the candidate. Interested candidates e-mail or fax their resumes to SkillSearch, which then faxes them on to you.

Corporate Organizing and Research Services

Corporate Organizing and Research Services, Inc. (CORS), located at www.cors.com, is another ERB with a wide range of recruiting services and price structures to choose from. The services range from receiving a report of potential candidates to having a CORS research professional phone the candidates directly to establish interest. For example, the CORSNet report provides detailed information on thirty professionals who meet the criteria in your job opening description. The report also provides current background data such as qualifications, experience, compensation, education, and home address. All professionals are polled to determine their interest in a job change in general and in your opportunity specifically.

CORS offers a guarantee that if you are not satisfied with the results, it will continue working on the assignment at no additional cost until you are satisfied. Some of its clients include the Frontier Corporation, Moore Business Forms, Office Depot, and Hewlett-Packard. CORS can be your confidential recruiting partner to tap into this area of networking. I believe you have the option for your company name to remain anonymous until there is a mutual interest between the job seeker and the company.

Resume-Link

Resume-Link has been providing MBA resumes to companies on diskette since 1990 and now has partnered with Restrak to offer an online search package. Resume-Link collects and organizes online resumes from top MBA programs and packs them into a single searchable resource called MBA QuickSearch. Resume-Link also pools resumes from some of the largest professional and engineering societies for you to tap into for a fee. You can learn more about QuickSearch or Restrak by logging onto their web site located at www.restrac.com.

Avoid the Bug

With resumes arriving at your desk by fax, zip drive, flip drive, zap mail, flap mail, snail mail, e-mail, html code, scanners, banners, and scammers, you need to think about the possibility of getting stung by a nasty bug carrying something as horrific as a virus. With little or no warning, these miniprograms can do irreversible damage to the data you rely on for your livelihood. They sneak in when you're not looking, and they sometimes go unnoticed for a while. Then all of a sudden you go to save a document and the system won't let you. You start to panic as you try to read the screen flashing something at you. You may see a skeleton face or a black bomb icon flashing at you. You may even start to see double—now you have two blinking bombs waiting to explode on your screen.

Soon you have an ugly skeleton fading in and out on your screen. Each time he reappears he is larger and more horrifying. The skeleton may even start talking to you, laughing at you — "Ha ha, you idiot, gotcha!" Or the bomb may explode at this point with the words "you're dead."

In a state of pure panic you reach for your phone. After several attempts, you finally connect with someone from the Help Desk. You request the best computer wizard available to come right away and check things out. The diagnosis? A virus on your desktop. Your life may never be the same again.

I may have exaggerated just a little here, but this is a very sore subject for me since a nasty virus was responsible for a near tragic end to this book. Some of the data had to be reentered and some were lost forever. Now, as a survivor of the Riper Virus, I make backups of my backups. Once you've been attacked by this evil, you vow always to protect yourself with a back-up, safely stored far away from your comfortable environment. Make sure you invest in up-to-date virus protection software to detect viruses and stand guard for you day and night. Hopefully, you are already in the habit of performing regular virus scans and backing up your data. If you aren't, you should know two things. First, as a recruiter or HR professional, you are a likely target for a virus programmer. Second, working online could increase your chances of encountering viruses.

So what exactly is a virus? In my more naive days I thought virus problems were glitches in software programs rather than manmade vengeful independent code written to run on a computer without your permission. Most viruses can also replicate themselves. The most dangerous type of virus is one capable of transmitting itself across networks and bypassing security systems. Viruses often are spread as a document file, typically attached to e-mail. Many job seekers create their resumes in Word and attach a copy to e-mails sent in response to job postings. Companies receive hundreds of resumes a day, making even accidental virus infection that much easier. Most virus infections are unintentional. Job seekers probably aren't even aware they are passing the virus on to their potential employers. The ones that do the most damage are the malicious viruses created by disgruntled employees. For example, if employees are denied raises, promotions, or benefits, they may strike back at whomever they perceive to be responsible. If you are in charge of human resources, that person could be you. Rejected candidates for high-tech job openings sometimes turn to viruses for revenge. Computer professionals are often adept at creating code, and those who find it difficult to express grievances through the proper channels sometimes rely on a virus as a way of expressing anger or rage. There are also some viruses out there aimed directly at Microsoft products. Whatever the reasons—jealousy, hatred, or disagreement with monopolizing business practices—Microsoft viruses are abundant.

There are many different types of viruses, and they are rapidly increasing in number. Some are benign and only give you a message on your screen, but others are far more devastating and are referred to as malignant viruses. These can damage your hard drive, cause your system to crash, and damage or corrupt files, resulting in lost data. The symptoms are not always the same. Your computer may just start acting up sporadically. If you suspect a virus, you should check out the virus help centers online, such as Symantec.com or drsolomon.com, to confirm that you have a virus and learn what you can do to get rid of it. Following are some indicators (found online at drsolomon.com) that can help you determine whether you have a virus or it is just a false alarm. Remember that these are just indicators; none of them provides conclusive proof that you definitely have a virus.

According to an antivirus package, several files on the computer are infected, all with the same virus.

It is a virus that is known to be "in the wild."

More than one antivirus package agrees that you have a virus.

Several COM and/or EXE files on your computer are all larger than they used to be, each by about the same amount.

Windows 95 refuses to use 32 bit disk access or 32 bit file access.

If you try to save a Word for Windows document (using File/Save As), the options are grayed out. You cannot select the drive, folder, or directory in which to save the file; and "Document Template" is the selected option in the "Save File as Type" box.

If Findvirus (from drsolomon.com) says that it has identified the virus, then it means that it has not just found a byte-signature; it means that it has check summed all the constant virus bytes, and they match the check sum in its database. So it's very unlikely to be a false alarm.

Here are some indicators that tell you nothing about the likelihood that you have a virus. (These are included here because many people think these are clear signs of a virus.)

Your hard disk doesn't work anymore
You're getting unusual graphics on your screen.
Your hard disk light seems to come on for no particular reason.
You just ran some downloaded software.

While the danger of being hit by a virus shouldn't be taken lightly, there is no need to overreact. Provided you take a few simple precautions, there is no reason you can't recruit online safely and free of viruses. Just make sure you have the latest antivirus software loaded onto your computer.

KEY CONCEPTS

>> Tool 1: Stay current—use free electronic newsletters and HR publications.

>> Tool 2: Let the software do all the work—the sit-back-and-wait approach; maximize your exposure through cross-posting services.

>> Tool 3: Shop around—fraud is everywhere on the net; get referrals and recommendations; know whom you are doing business with.

>> Tool 4: Get statistics—use software to verify links and statistics online.

>> Tool 5: Throw out the old rules of recruiting—treat job seekers like potential customers, with respect, courtesy, and superior customer service.

>> Tool 6: Manage the scarcity—just-in-time recruiting; put your job seeker's shoes on.

>> Tool 7: Seek out diversity—visit and register with organizations targeting specific minorities and industries you are recruiting.

>> Tool 8: Manage the results—use software to help you manage and track the results.

>> Tool 9: Outsource—find out who can do it better and more cost-effectively.

>> Tool 10: Avoid the bug—invest in virus protection software; be cautious and aware of how viruses can penetrate your files.

Part Two

Best Places
on the Internet
for Online Recruiting

Chapter Five

The Best
of the Freebies

Many web sites offered free resume searching and free job postings when they first opened up shop. For example, Headhunter offered free job postings and resume searches until June 1999. Many sites have realized the need to keep up with the marketing campaigns of other leading job banks and must charge a fee to help offset the millions of dollars they spend on recruitment advertising. However, some sites are still free. If you're one of those people who say, "You get what you pay for"—when it comes to online recruiting, this is not totally valid. This chapter will show you where you can post your job openings for free or at a very reasonable cost. You also will learn about some great places to source resumes. You will learn where you can search resumes online for free and receive fresh resumes in your e-mail or regular mailbox, all for free.

Receive Fresh Resumes in Your E-mail Every Day

As you already know, e-mail is a very popular communication method and many recruiters and employers prefer to receive an electronic version of potential candidates' resumes. Because of this, many services have sprung up to accommodate and complement this preferred way of recruiting. I will discuss some pioneers in this arena to provide you with enough information for you to decide if this is a service you could benefit from. It is important to remember that resume distribution services charge the job seeker, not the employer or recruiter. This is quite the opposite of most online recruiting services, where the job seeker receives the service, tools, and advice absolutely free. All the major sites offer free services to job seekers in order to attract them and keep them coming back; this is how they stay competitive. The revenues are generated from banner advertisements and the fees charged to recruiters or employers for posting jobs or searching resumes. You may be wondering how a service can charge the job seeker when job seekers can get almost everything they want for free. Well, these services are targeted to serious job seekers (not passive ones), who are paying between $50 and $200 to have their resumes distributed to thousands of recruiters. The idea is great and these services are quite successful. These job seekers also seem to like the idea of their resumes being exposed to the maximum number of recruiters. Recruiters can start receiving these resumes in their e-mail for free.

RESUME BLASTER

Resume Blaster (www.resumeblaster.com) is one of the premier resume distribution services on the Internet. There are many imitators, but I believe this is one of the best targeted services. Various job seekers have told me that the people at Resume Blaster offer superior customer service and they've had tremendous response after using this service. One job seeker, an experienced MBA looking to relocate to Arizona, told me he had received over a hundred e-mails and phone calls from recruiters and headhunters after using this service. Another job seeker received approximately forty e-mails and phone calls within a two-week period. Former headhunters and recruiters familiar with the recruitment business developed this site. They have built a distribution system that blasts candidates' resumes to more than 2,500 recruiters across the country. They charge a reasonable price to the job seeker and the service is free to recruiters and hiring managers. You may cancel your free subscription at any time or change your requests—for example, you may choose to receive only resumes from a specific category of candidates, such as engineers.

RESUME XPRESS

Resume Xpress, a service of Online Solutions, Inc., is located online at www.resumexpress.com and has all the bells and whistles you would expect from a resume distribution service, plus advanced search criteria. For example, when you enter search criteria, not only does it search the candidates in its current database, but your search remains "live" on the database, allowing every subsequently entered resume that matches your search criteria to be sent to your e-mail address automatically—all at no cost to you whatsoever. The candidate pays for the service at the time the resume is entered into the system. The advanced search capabilities ResumeXpress offers are very similar to those offered by Resume Scout from America's Job Bank (to be discussed later in the chapter).

EMPLOYMENT ZONE

Employment Zone, located at www.employmentzone.com, distributes job seekers' resumes to over 1,500 locations on the web. This site is similar to Resume Blaster. You decide whether you want to contact the candidate via e-mail or by phone. Distribution sites such as this are a great tool for companies with many offices across the country. You can find staff for these distant offices a bit more easily by signing up for one of these resume distribution services. For more information regarding Employment Zone, you can contact the company at this e-mail address: info@employmentzone.com.

Uncle Sam May Be Your Best Recruiting Friend

During my days of researching web sites that promised free postings or free resume searching, I wondered why anyone would do this. After all, isn't the bottom line making money? You must make money if you are to survive and compete. Well, I found out the sites offering free resume searches and/or job postings *are* making money—they're just doing it in a roundabout way. The sites that follow, America's Job Bank and the Defense Outplacement Referral System (DORS) are funded by the U.S. government and have been operating successfully for quite a few years now. They are both absolutely free and easy to use. I was skeptical at first, thinking that anything involving the government must be layers thick with bureaucracy and complications. I was dead wrong.

AMERICA'S JOB BANK

America's Job Bank (www.ajb.dni.us) is offered by our friends at the U.S. Department of Labor and is one of the largest and longest-running Internet job sites in existence. This job posting site and resume talent bank is absolutely free—sort of. I'm afraid our tax dollars somewhere along the line paid for the computer geniuses, the systems administrators, the designers, the office folks, and the whole staff. Actually, employers fund America's Job Bank and each state's employment service program through unemployment insurance taxes.

Most of the jobs listed on America's Job Bank are full-time listings and in the private sector. The job openings come from all over the country and represent all types of work, from professional and technical to blue collar, from management to clerical and sales. If you have a notion that laid-off workers are the only ones utilizing this site, you're wrong. Doctors, lawyers, computer specialists, and people from all walks of life use this site. The resumes listed with America's Job Bank are from candidates with a wide range of skills and experience in all types of employment fields. You can confirm this by visiting the home page for America's Job Bank on the web. There are over 500,000 resumes at this site. You can contact candidates by just clicking on their e-mail address to zap them a personal message about your job opening.

We've known for a while now that the number of openings in the IT labor market far exceed the number of available skilled job seekers. Unfortunately, this trend is predicted to continue over the next five years. According to the U.S. Bureau of Labor Statistics, computer scientists, computer engineers, and systems analysts are expected to be the three fastest-growing occupations through 2006.

I believe employers need to lower their standards just a little and start offering more jobs to their existing staff or recent college graduates. Quite often, an internal training program such as on-the-job training or mentoring employees in-house is the better alternative. Why not invest some time and money to develop and train employees already on your payroll to meet your current and future needs rather than trying to hold out for the perfect candidate? I have seen companies allow a job order to go unfilled for a year and sometimes longer due to their refusal to lower their hiring standards and minimum job requirements. I know every employer prefers the candidate with the exact match of qualifications for the job opening and holds out as long as possible to find that perfect candidate. What is the perfect IT candidate? Someone with a minimum of five years' work experience in a related position, proficient in every known programming language, and with multiple degrees in engineering and computer science. In reality, most recruiters don't have a file drawer overflowing with such dream candidates. So what do we do about this crisis situation? You're already taking the first step in the right direction by learning more about online recruiting and tapping into the reservoir of passive job seekers just waiting for the right opportunity to change jobs.

The good news is that more experienced programmers are entering their resumes into online resume banks, such as America's Job Bank, with the intention of finding a new and challenging career opportunity. I thought I had died and gone to heaven when I first stumbled across this site with all those free resumes.

The only downside of this site is that it competes with commercial sites that advertise during the Super Bowl and with large job boards taking out full-page advertisements in major newspapers and employment magazines. Given the competition, the high number of job seekers and employers it has attracted is astonishing. I have yet to see a full-page ad for this great site and probably never will. Why? Because America's Job Bank is a service, not a business trying to turn a profit. However, on the upside, because this is a public employment site operating in every state, it provides one of the largest labor exchange services for employers and job seekers. This network consists of 1,800 offices throughout the United States. This public employment service has been in existence for more than sixty years, helping people and jobs find each other. As of July 9, 1999, this site had 998,974 job seekers registered and 859,374 jobs. These statistics are updated daily and can be viewed on America's Job Bank's home page. The following information was taken from the site's employer information page.

Since 1979 the states have cooperated to exchange information in order to offer employers national exposure for their job openings. In the spring of 1998 the additional service of posting resumes from job seekers was initiated. Publicizing job listings on a national basis has helped employers recruit the employees they need to help their businesses succeed, while providing the American labor force with an increased number of opportunities to find work and realize their career goals.

America's Job Bank's computerized network links state employment service offices to provide job seekers with the largest pool of active job opportunities available and nationwide exposure for their resumes. For employers it provides rapid, national exposure for job openings and an easily accessible pool of candidates. In addition to the Internet, the job openings and resumes found in America's Job Bank are available on computer systems in public libraries, colleges and universities, high schools, shopping malls, transition offices on military bases worldwide, and other places of public access.

One measurement tool I feel is a benefit to this great site is the ability to track and monitor your job postings. You can post unlimited job postings to this site and search as many resumes as you like. You can go to the employer's page and select reports, where the system will show you every active or closed posting you have as well as how many people have viewed and responded to your posting. If the number of views is twenty-five, that may mean the same person looked at the ad twenty-five times, but more than likely it means that twenty-five different job seekers searched the site and read your advertisement. I am generally skeptical about the accuracy of online view counters because technical geniuses can play with the programs to show whatever numbers they choose. However, I'm convinced America's Job Bank has no reason to inflate these numbers. Additionally, from my own experience using this site, I believe the numbers are extremely accurate.

As with all government programs, there is some paperwork involved in registering to use this site; however, there is no cost for registration. During the registration process, you will be able to choose the method that best suits your employment needs, technical capabilities, and volume. You may even qualify for automated job postings so you won't have to reenter any of your job requirements. Additionally, you can indicate your preference for the way you want to receive job seeker information. You may post your company name, address, and phone number, or you may request to remain anonymous. If you choose the latter option, all the resumes will first be sent to the Department of Labor's offices and then sent to you for review.

You will also be able to update, modify, close, extend, and archive job postings as often as you require. All orders are open for thirty days. You can extend the job posting for another thirty days. If you archive the job, it is removed from the database but can be recalled in the future.

After posting a job order, you can then elect to (1) post additional job order(s), (2) post another job order based on information in this job, or (3) search for resumes based on information in this job. The second and third options listed here are great time savers because they eliminate the need to post the same information more than once and allow you to search resumes as soon as you've posted a job. For example, if you have ten job postings and all of them start and end with the same standard company information, you don't have to retype or paste anything. The previous ad's basic information is automatically added to your next ad, saving you time and data entry keystrokes. Additionally, if you are an employer, most state offices will enter your job openings at this site for you. If you are a third-party recruiter, I believe you will have to handle the data inputting yourself. Also, if you are the employer, the job services division at state offices will prescreen candidates for you, handle all the incoming faxes and mailings, and send you only the resumes of candidates meeting your minimum qualifications.

This site also provides an Advanced Resume Search feature that allows you to enter specific words, text, or other search criteria (such as location or education) that further refine the original text you want to see on suitable candidates' resumes. You can even indicate whether you want an exact spelling match or variations are acceptable. The system will apply the additional criteria only after it has narrowed the field to resumes that have the initial words or phrases you have selected. For example, you can enter "AS 400" and "Database Administrator." These words will become part of the search logic used to narrow the field of candidates. You can also refine your query by geographic location. If you specify a particular city, for example, the name of that city must appear at least once in each of the resumes returned from the database. You can enter a zip code to narrow your search to a very specific geographic location. You can also decide how large a radius you want the database to search—for example, a five-, twenty-five-, or fifty-mile radius across a particular zip code. This option is handy if you have quite a few smaller towns surrounding a large metropolitan area. Another option is to select up to three states rather than limiting your search to a narrow geographic area. You can enter general skills required instead of location. You can use a fairly general word or phrase for the initial search and, if that results in too many responses, refine the term with more specifics. With this method you eventually narrow your results to just a handful of qualified candidates.

This system has a timesaving feature called the Resume Scout, which automatically e-mails you any time a new job seeker enters into the Talent Bank a resume matching your job requirements. This is a great sit-back-and-wait approach. You can request automatic e-mail notification every day, every week, or at any interval you prefer.

DEFENSE OUTPLACEMENT REFERRAL SYSTEMS (DORS)

Defense Outplacement Referral Systems (DORS), located at http://dod.jobsearch.org, is another great free government site. The Defense Authorization Act of 1991 (Public Law 101-510) required that the secretary of defense provide employment assistance to separating military service members and their spouses. Therefore, DORS is also referred to as Operation Transition.

The Office of the Secretary of Defense and the U.S. military services (Army, Navy, Marine Corps, Air Force, and Coast Guard) joined together to design automated programs to link employers and job seekers around the world. DORS, a resume registry and referral system, is one of those programs. The Transition Bulletin Board (TBB), a database of employment ads and other career information, is another. Employers and recruiters have the option to post jobs online to the TBB.

More than 22,000 employers, from small businesses to Fortune 500 companies, have registered to use Operation Transition (DORS). Highly trained military personnel and federal civilian employees and their spouses complete DORS applications and review TBB want ads. They possess a wide variety of education, training, and experience. During 1998 more than two million DORS resumes were sent to employers — and DORS keeps growing. The demand for DORS resumes has spurred pilot programs with other downsizing federal agencies, which are expected to participate soon. Employers have access to a vast pool of highly qualified employees.

How does DORS work? Job seekers enter their qualifications and job location preferences into computers at one of more than 300 transition offices worldwide. The information is transmitted to the DORS database at the Defense Manpower Data Center in Seaside, California. Once employers have registered with Operation Transition, they request resumes based on the type of job vacancy and its geographic location. DORS makes the match, and employers view resumes immediately.

I have used this site numerous times and have been impressed with the quick response, customer service, and quality of resumes. I can phone in a resume request on a Monday and by Wednesday morning I will have a hundred fresh resumes express mailed to me free of charge. Now that is what I call service without a price tag. Please note, effective April 15, 1999, DORS discontinued the touch-tone telephone method for employers to request resumes. Instead, all resume requests are handled via its superior web site and can be downloaded on the spot. This method is quicker and allows you to view resumes online or have resumes e-mailed or faxed to you. The system is pretty sophisticated, but easy to use. You can manage the results online via the web site, print out your own hard copies, or contact the candidates via e-mail. To request resumes online, all you have to do is enter two fields — the job code and the zip code. I like to send all resumes to my online briefcase folder and then narrow the field further by doing a page-view search for particular key words or skills sets I'm looking for.

Some of the statistics provided by DORS are in the following Fast Facts chart.

All separating service members will have received military training in their areas of expertise equal in value to hundreds of thousands of dollars in the private sector economy. These former service members will provide employers with the opportunity to hire top-notch professionals in virtually every category—electronics, equipment repair, computer programming, communications, healthcare, accounting, finance, and many more. They bring a willingness to work, an ability to get along with all kinds of people, and a sense of discipline to the civilian workforce. DORS clients Aerotek, Inc., and Allied Security have provided online testimonials on the DORS web site recommending this service to others.

The second-best thing about using DORS is the flexibility of the job seekers. The majority of job seekers from this system are in transition and separating from the military. They usually don't have a home to sell and are very open to relocating to just about anywhere a good job opportunity presents itself. These skilled, disciplined candidates are seriously looking for a permanent job opportunity to start their civilian careers. I highly recommend this site to anyone in the field of recruitment, contract or permanent. The system is divided into job-specific categories from clerical to scientists (remember, your tax dollars already paid for it, so you might as well use it).

Online Services for Posting and Searching Resumes

There are always new sites popping up and claiming they are superior to all the others. Sometimes it's hard to know whom to believe about which services are really the best. I've been researching online recruitment services for almost three years now. If I can't judge from my own personal experience, I will often rely on other expert opinions in the online recruiting field—other experienced recruiters, survey results, or industry awards. Even then, it's difficult to decide who's the best. In Appendix C, there's a directory of recruiting web sites with letter rankings by experts as to quality. Ultimately you need to judge for yourself what service is best for you and your unique business. I often rely on statistics posted on major sites. Sometimes the numbers speak for themselves.

HEADHUNTER

Headhunter (www.headhunter.net) is another top-notch resume searching site. Until June 1999, recruiters and employers could post all the job openings they wanted to for free at Headhunter. Now each new job posting costs $20. This minimal cost is still a great value for such a successful job posting site. If you like to search resumes online, this site offers fresh resumes (never more than ninety days old) to search for free to your heart's content. Some statistics on this site are listed in the Fast Facts charts at right.

Over 140,000 job listings and nearly 250,000 resumes? These are not old resumes, either—this site notifies job seekers when their resumes are about to expire and gives them the option to update the resume or lose it from the database. You can find candidates in all industries on this site—from across town and across the continent. This site is also user-friendly—you can view resumes with the click of a button and send an e-mail to a potential candidate with another click. This site has been around for quite some time and generates most of its revenue from banner advertisements and by offering upgrades (fees paid to increase visibility by sorting

FAST FACTS

Headhunter Statistics as of October 1999

Total jobs. 140,360
Total resumes. 247,778
VIP resume reserve 32,537
Daily users 120,531

FAST FACTS

Breakdown of Popular Job Categories

Computer jobs 96,690
Engineering jobs 18,775
Accounting/financial jobs . 19,491
Sales/marketing jobs. . . 15,942

job postings or resumes according to their upgrade value) to employers and job seekers.

YAHOO

Is there anyone who hasn't heard of Yahoo? My mother is sixty-five years old and is just starting to become interested in the Internet. My husband and I helped her pick out a computer and hooked her up to the Internet in late 1998. When she was first exploring the web, she was confused about a lot of things—but not about Yahoo. Even though she mispronounced its name (Yoho instead of Yahoo), she knew this leader in the search world was something she needed to pay attention to. Not too many employers or recruiters are aware that Yahoo has a free job posting service. I wasn't, until just last year when another recruiter told me about it (or maybe it was my mother). Yahoo helps job seekers, employers, and recruiters hook up to fill job openings. You can access this site at www.yahoo.com.

At Yahoo's main web page, all you have to do is click on Classifieds and then on Employment. Yahoo recently added a (free) batch feed service— if you have over 100 job postings you can batch feed them all at once to save time. This is an excellent source of free job postings and is widely used by active job seekers. Yahoo is also popular for its free classifieds and attracts many passive candidates. When they go online to check out cars or computers, they are tempted to check out new jobs as well. This is an easy-to-use site—you can experiment with your first job ad at this site almost effortlessly. As of December 1999 Yahoo had more than 360,000 jobs posted. If you put this book down right now you can try it out.

BRIDGEPATH

In a survey by Fred Jandt and Mary Nemnich, authors of *Cyberspace Resume Kit* (1998), only a handful of sites received a five-star rating: Bridgepath, Careerfile, Career Mart, Monster.com, and Transition Assistance Online. Jandt and Nemnich evaluated the sites on numerous criteria, such as stability, cost to job seeker and employer, number of resumes compared to number of employers using the bank, confidentiality, sophistication of search options, and ease of entering and using the site. Here's why Bridgepath received a five-star rating.

FAST FACTS

Bridgepath Vital Statistics as of July 1999

>> 100% of Bridgepath members have e-mail addresses

>> 99% have a college degree or are currently working toward a college degree

>> Bridgepath has members from over 800 colleges

>> 12% are in the San Francisco Bay Area

>> 10% are in the New York area

>> There are over 200,000 members, and more than 3,000 new members join each week

>> Member composition:

Information technology: 21%	Sales: 6%
Engineering: 17%	Marketing: 6%
Management: 16%	Clerical: 4%
Accounting: 14%	Manufacturing: 1%
Life sciences: 14%	Other: 3%

Source: Bridgepath web page

Bridgepath (www.bridgepath.com) provides a full-service, 100 percent Internet-based contact management and customer relationship management system for recruiting and staffing firms: the Bridgepath Recruiters Network. Bridgepath was founded in 1996 as one of the first Internet job boards primarily focusing on college graduates. As you can see from the above Fast Facts chart, 99 percent of Bridgepath job seekers are college graduates or are working toward a college degree. Bridgepath.com has grown into a site offering opportunities to over 200,000 candidates from around the country, and over 2,000 employers have used Bridgepath services. The site has formed strategic partnerships with Kennedy Information, AIRS, Recruiters Online Network, Inc. (RON), and other key recruitment organizations and services. The Bridgepath Recruiters Network eliminates many tedious recruiting tasks, including cold calling, finding phone numbers, reading resumes, setting up interviews, and tending to IT issues. The Bridgepath system assists third-party recruiters with relationship building, contact tracking, research, business expansion, and sales management. Bridgepath also allows employers and recruiters to post jobs for free with an easy-to-use online template for job postings.

CAREER MAGAZINE

Career Magazine (www.careermag.com), another leader in the field, is noted for the wide variety of articles posted online from various recruiters and for expert online advice for the job seeker. In May of 1998 it posted an article I wrote entitled "Your Resume Gets You the Interview, Your Portfolio Gets You the Job!" I received an enormous amount of correspondence about this feature, whereas other online articles I've written for other sites haven't received nearly as big a response. In addition to articles, Career Magazine also has a career forum, "Ask Allison," e-mails, a resume bank, and job postings. Searching the resume database cost nothing until late 1998. Now employers and recruiters can search a free database of older resumes (sixty days or more) or pay for fresh resumes.

The cost of posting job openings varies depending on the package you select—one job posting costs less than $135. You can select from a wide variety of pricing packages to fit your staffing requirements. The available packages are as follows (includes searching fresh resumes).

Brass package: up to 5 concurrent job postings
Copper package: up to 15 concurrent job postings
Bronze package: up to 30 concurrent job postings
Silver package: up to 75 concurrent job postings
Gold package: unlimited concurrent job postings

NET-TEMPS

Net-Temps, located at www.net-temps.com, was designed specifically for the staffing industry. Job seekers can search jobs, recruiters can search resumes, and employers can hire temps online. This site also features a free thirty-day trial for recruiters to post job openings to over 400 top-rated web sites. It also offers a free service for job seekers searching for their ideal job on a national, state, or city level. Net-Temps' resume bank announces the job seeker's availability to thousands of staffing services with one entry by the candidate. This is a very attractive feature as candidates can expect to receive many phone calls, e-mails, and interviews within a week of submission. As a member of Net-Temps you will receive a daily list of candidates that have applied in the last twenty-four hours. Your user name and password enable you to search the spider resume bank where a robot has indexed virtually every resume on the web—over 225,000 at last count. Online guided tours of this site are also definitely worth checking out.

INTERNET CAREER CONNECTION

In 1989, Internet Career Connection (ICC) created the first career guidance agency to operate 100 percent online. Since its inception ICC has helped millions of individuals enhance their career development or secure employment, in addition to helping thousands of companies and recruiters find new candidates for employment. From its Internet web site and its Career Center Forum at America Online, ICC services more than a million customers each month. There are over 50,000 resumes on average in the database. ICC is located at www.iccweb.com.

OTHER RESUME DATABASES WORTH CHECKING OUT

A+ Online Resumes (www.ol-resume.com/category.htm): You can search for free by industry and by geographic location. The database is growing daily and worth checking out.

America's TV Job Network (www.tvjobnet.com): You can search for free by industry and position. You'll find lots of media types in this database.

Career America (www.careeramerica.com): There are lots of entry-level jobs to search for free.

Engineering Jobs (www.engineeringjobs.com): Here are engineering resumes to search for free.

Future Access Resume Inquiry (www.futureaccess.com): Biotech, hardware and software engineering, sales and marketing, and human resource resumes can be found at this site.

Resume Net (www.resumenet.com): You can find thousands of free resumes in over sixty categories here.

All You Need to Know About
Usenets and Newsgroups

User networks have been popular with special interest groups on the Internet for a long time. Most of them are run by individuals or nonprofit groups out of their passion for networking or sharing information. They are not run by businesses trying to turn a profit. One of the reasons Usenets became so popular was because they were (and still are) free to use. They were one of the first places for job seekers to hear about job opportunities. Recently, however, Usenets have been inundated with unsolicited job postings. Therefore, some of the more popular Usenets have been putting a stop to free posting to their newsgroups. The poor web site administrators of these Usenets had to handle thousands of job postings (with much duplication). The administration was a nightmare, and users were also complaining about the information overload. These Usenets have been in existence for years because individuals with similar interests and knowledge can share information here easily, in a friendly, low-key atmosphere. At first they may have enjoyed receiving notification of jobs, but when all kinds of other (mostly intrusive) information started showing up, the site administrators felt they had to put up blockades. Some have even invested in software to block unwelcome sales pitches.

If you were to post a get-rich-quick scheme in one of these newsgroups, there is a good chance you would get flamed. Flaming is similar to road rage, but here the weapon is the printed word. I'm making this point to stress the importance of minding your manners and using proper "netiquette" if you decide to post to these groups. You want to make sure you don't post a job order for a chemist position in Texas on the Phoenix newsgroup board. Filters for screening out all the unwanted job postings and ads are becoming more available to users. Some staffing firms seem to believe that if they post the same jobs to a Usenet group fifty times a day they will get better results. In my opinion, this results only in annoying users with unwanted and unsolicited information.

DEJA

Deja specifically targets newsgroup forums and does a pretty good job of making sense of the chaos. It has a speedy power search tool that enables you to search hundreds of Usenets according to your key word parameters. Prior to June of 1999, Deja was called Deja News. With the new name came some redesigning of its services. It has a unique feature called the Deja Tracker that enables you to find out what new resumes have been posted without actually returning to the web site again. The Deja Tracker can tag a conversation and send you e-mail notification when new messages are posted. If you really like lurking around newsgroups and forums, you can also subscribe to a newsgroup. You will receive e-mail, daily summaries, full-text digests, or messages posted to your particular newsgroup. Deja also uses a filter so you won't receive intrusive advertisements or spam. Spam has been a prevalent online problem. Congress has been passing laws, but it seems as difficult to control online junk mail as it is to control post office junk mail. The site is located on the web at www.dejanews.com.

RECRUITUSA

Another site that does a great job of sorting through all the free resumes is RecruitUSA at www.recruitusa.com. The RecruitUSA resume database is composed of data submitted by job seekers to Internet newsgroups. This site has similar search capabilities to Deja's and is also a great source of free resumes. You should choose one or the other because the same candidates will probably pop up in your search queries as they both extract resumes from newsgroups. Recruit USA also has other services such as job postings and cross postings. Both Deja and RecruitUSA are worth checking out.

TO LURK OR NOT TO LURK IN NEWSGROUPS

More and more recruiters say they are finding the passive job seekers in targeted newsgroups and they need these passive job seekers (especially technically proficient ones) in order to do their job well. There are online recruiting experts who would challenge the concept that hanging out around newsgroups and Usenet chats is the only way to recruit passive job seekers—especially in the highly technical areas. I can't argue the fact that you will find a talented group of professionals at Usenets. However, what is the risk of intruding? I am a proponent of building long-lasting relationships and discarding any tricks to entice job seekers with bait-and-switch tactics. If I were to join a systems analyst discussion group on networking to announce a great job opportunity, I would either get flamed or be ignored. The silent treatment is often a successful online tactic to overcome unwelcome intruders in these private places. Pretending someone isn't in the chat room or discussion by totally ignoring the intruder works better than flaming. You could be very tactful and use the most eloquent words to express your desire to help the discussion participants find a great job opportunity, but it wouldn't matter because you would still be in the wrong place at the wrong time. You could take a low-key approach and lurk around these groups learning the trade talk, when the trade shows are in town. Or you could review posted discussions from previous chat sessions. If you have time to do this, great! You are improving your base knowledge and gaining a more in-depth understanding of the candidates you are trying to recruit. However, I advise you to avoid joining in these discussions unless you, too, are an expert in the particular area and can offer good advice.

Newsgroups are an essential component to add to your online recruiting tool kit. Following is a list of some top user groups where you can search resumes for free. There are actually thousands of these groups that you can check for job seekers in specific locations or with targeted skills. Some recruiters have great success using this method, but I don't frequently use it myself. Your decision may depend on how important it is for you to target job seekers in a specific geographic area or possessing a specific skill. You should also note that although most of these sites offer free job posting, some sites are putting an end to this. They've already started to halt automatic, multiple job postings from major job boards (such as Dice and others), but you should be able to post jobs individually to most of these sites.

CHART 7	NEWSGROUP SITES
Newsgroup	Description
alt.jobs	Jobs in Atlanta, Georgia
aus.jobs	Jobs available and wanted in Australia
austin.jobs	Jobs in Austin, Texas
ba.jobs.contract	Contract jobs in the San Francisco Bay Area
Ba.jobs.misc.	Job market in the San Francisco Bay Area
Ba.jobs.offered	Job postings in the San Francisco Bay Area
Bionet.jobs	Scientific jobs
Can.jobs	Jobs in Canada
Cle.jobs	Jobs in Cleveland, Ohio
co.jobs	Jobs in Colorado
ct.jobs	Jobs in Connecticut
dc.jobs	Jobs in Washington, D.C.
Fl.jobs	Jobs in Florida
Houston.jobs.offered	Houston employment
Ia.jobs	Jobs in Iowa
il.jobs.offered	Jobs in Illinois
in.jobs	Jobs in Indiana
ithaca.jobs	Jobs in Ithaca, New York
la.jobs	Jobs in Louisiana
mi.jobs	Jobs in Michigan
Milw.jobs	Jobs in Milwaukee
Misc.jobs.contract	Discussions about contract labor
Misc.jobs.misc.	Employment, workplaces, careers
Misc.jobs.offered	Job announcements
Misc.jobs.offered.entry	Entry-level job openings
Misc.jobs.resumes	Postings of resumes

CHART 7	NEWSGROUP SITES continued
Newsgroup	Description
Ne.jobs	Jobs in New England
nebr.jobs	Jobs in Nebraska
nh.jobs	Jobs in New Hampshire
ny.jobs	Jobs in New Jersey
nyc.jobs	Jobs in New York City
nyc.jobs.offered	Jobs in New York City
nyc.jobs.wanted	Jobs wanted in New York City
oh.jobs	Jobs in Ohio
pa.jobs.offered	Jobs in Pennsylvania
pa.jobs.wanted	Jobs wanted in Pennsylvania
pgh.jobs.offered	Jobs in Pittsburgh
phl.jobs.offered	Jobs in Philadelphia
Phx.jobs.wanted	Jobs in Phoenix
seattle.jobs.offered	Jobs in Seattle
seattle.jobs.wanted	Jobs wanted in Seattle
Su.jobs	Stanford University community want ads
Triangle.jobs	Jobs in North Carolina
Tx.jobs	Jobs in Texas
Uiuc.cs.jobs	Computer science–related jobs
us.jobs	Jobs in United States
us.jobs.contract	Contract jobs in United States
ut.jobs	Jobs in Utah
va.jobs	Jobs in Virginia
vegas.jobs	Jobs in Las Vegas

KEY CONCEPTS

>> Receive free resumes in your e-mail by using services such as Resume Blaster, Resume Xpress, and Employment Zone.

>> Utilize government-sponsored sites such as America's Job Bank from the U.S. Department of Labor and the Defense Outplacement Referral System (DORS).

>> Check out popular commercial sites that offer free or low-cost resume searching or job postings—for example, Headhunter, Yahoo, Bridgepath, Career Magazine, Net-Temps, Internet Career Connection, and others.

>> Utilize free Usenets and newsgroups to post job openings and announcements of job fairs and other events. Always practice proper "netiquette" when online. Don't be intrusive, and don't join discussions unless you can contribute knowledge or information of use to the members. Don't post a job to a Usenet unless you are sure this is allowed.

Chapter Six

Comparisons of Leading Web Sites

You already have the tools and strategies to assist you in online recruiting. Now you have to decide where to recruit for new talent. To help you decide among the thousands of sites available, I've placed a chart listing ten questions to ask prior to selecting a recruitment site at the end of this chapter. Internet recruiting is mushrooming and new sites are popping up almost daily. Read on to learn which of the thousands of online recruiting sites are leading the way.

The Best of the Best

So who's the best? Well, it depends on the survey you happen to review at any given time. In the never-static Internet environment the top ten change quite often, but some of the leaders have managed to stay in the top ten ranks for some time. According to Internet Business Network's (IBN) 1999 Electronic Recruiting Index survey, the following sites are ranked in the top ten.

I'm betting you've heard of some of these sites—unless you skipped "The Best of the Freebies" (Chapter 5). I mentioned Yahoo, Headhunter, and America's Job Bank there because all three of them are free or low-cost, superior recruitment sites. The other sites also have been around for a while, and in case you haven't heard about them, I've listed a brief summary of their services.

CHART 8	IBN'S TOP TEN RECRUITMENT WEB SITES	
1. CareerMosaic		6. America's Job Bank
2. Monster.com		7. Online Career Center*
3. AltaVista		8. Wall Street Journal
4. Yahoo Classifieds		9. Recruiters Online Network
5. Headhunter		10. E-Span (currently JobOptions)

*Officially joined with Monster.com in 1999

Source: Internet Business Network's 1999 Electronic Recruiting Index

CAREERMOSAIC

CareerMosaic (www.careermosaic.com), the number one site with IBN, has won hundreds of industry awards. This site is known for its massive exposure, superior service, and resume database. You can search ResumeCM for free if you belong to a member company. Over 60,000 resumes are posted exclusively on ResumeCM. In August of 1998 CareerMosaic initiated a paid subscription plan for recruiters who wish to search the ResumeCM database for job seekers' resumes. A six-month subscription costs around $600 and a twelve-month subscription costs about $1,000. Job seekers can still post their resumes to ResumeCM free of charge. At last check, this site received over 300,000 queries every day. Career-Mosaic's objective is to get job seekers to return to its site as often as possible so it can impress employers with the sheer number of visitors (or "hits"). This

FAST FACTS

CareerMosaic has:

>> Job openings: 100,000+ (as of January 2000)

>> Hits in a month: 56.9 million (October 1999)

>> Daily queries to jobs database: +474,000

>> Resumes on ResumeCM: 135,000+ at any given time

>> Visitors in a month: 4.5 million+ (October 1999)

Source: Nielsen-I/PRO (an independent site auditor)

a large recruitment advertising firm that really knows how to advertise. I believe CareerMosaic will continue to be one of the most visible contenders in the online recruitment arena. Some statistics are listed in the Fast Facts chart at left to give you an idea of the site's magnitude.

MONSTER.COM

Monster (www.monster.com) is one of the best-known sites. Monster.com (formally called MonsterBoard) is a flagship product of the Interactive Division of TMP Worldwide, the fourteenth-largest ad agency in the United States. It has won numerous awards and has set up alliances with so many others that its web site has a drop-down menu just to list them all. One partner is the well-known Online Career Center, which joined in January 1999 to create an even bigger Monster.com site. Monster.com is also known for its innovative job search agent, offered free to job seekers and member companies. Some of the companies advertising on this site are Sun Microsystems, Rand, Silicon Graphics, AT&T, GTE, HBO, BellSouth, Ratheon, Coopers & Lybrand, Microsoft, Blockbuster, Fidelity, Nike, Arthur Andersen, Compaq, and MCI. Monster.com also has a resume database called Resume City, which employers can search with unlimited usage. Employers can also activate the resume search agent called Cruiter, which will notify them of a candidate match, similar to the service offered to job seekers. This is a great tool for busy recruiters with many job openings. This wonderful service with all the bells and whistles doesn't come free. Monster.com charges $225 per posting for single job postings. It has a wide variety of customized packages to fit companies of every size.

At one time, Monster.com did not allow third-party firms access to the resume database—you had to be hiring for your own company—but this isn't the case anymore. I'm sure this management decision was influenced by harassment from some third-party agents posing as recruiters for reputable companies. I don't want to offend anyone reading this, but some headhunters have given the entire executive search business a bad rap due to their unscrupulous behavior. Monster.com management forced third parties out of the game entirely until they realized that third parties made up a good portion of their revenue. So now, anyone with a job order and a paid subscription can search Monster.com's massive resume bank and use all its cool automatic tools.

Job banks' real customers are job seekers who use their services free of charge. Human resource folks are paying top dollar to find and recruit these job seekers. Monster.com has done an excellent job of ensuring that job seekers have every possible tool at their fingertips when they are visiting this site. It also does its best to police unscrupulous behavior and allow only credible recruiters with "real" jobs access to its resume database.

One feature available to job seekers is the Personal Job Agent, which works around the clock to help job seekers find the right job. If I'm not mistaken, the Monster.com site was one of the first to offer this feature, which has now become standard on most job sites. The Personal Job Agent is a free service for all job seekers and is simple to use. Monster.com has been around since 1994. That's ancient in Internet time. In my opinion, this site will stay in the forefront in the next millennium and must be bookmarked.

ALTAVISTA

You can find the highly rated AltaVista site at www.altavista.com. You just have to click on the Careers button on its main home page and follow the links to view jobs or resumes. Like most search engines, AltaVista provides information according to your search criteria. That's why you should try to become proficient at using very specific key words to search for what you need. If you specify the word *resume* in your search this will ensure that you receive only resumes in the title. For example, if you key in "+title:resume" in the key word box, AltaVista's search engine will search for resumes. If you wanted to target your search to just resumes with the words *Unix* and *New York* in the text, you would type in "+title:resume+Unix+,NY".

YAHOO, HEADHUNTER, AMERICA'S JOB BANK

These three sites (rated 4, 5, and 6, respectively) were discussed in Chapter 5. They are all free or low-cost sites, and I forecast that in the foreseeable future all three of them will remain in the top ten vying for the lead position.

ONLINE CAREER CENTER

As I mentioned earlier, Online Career Center (OCC), formerly located at www.occ.com, officially joined with Monster.com in January 1999. They are no longer two separate entities, but one operating under the name Monster.com.

THE WALL STREET JOURNAL

The *Wall Street Journal* has a top-notch career site (www.careers.wsj.com) that attracts all types of job seekers (passive and not so passive) and that isn't just for financial folks. It attracts job seekers from management, IT, banking, manufacturing, communications, engineering, and other areas.

This site has been in the forefront of leading job sites mainly due to the powerful editorial resources of the *Wall Street Journal* and *National Business Employment Weekly.* Job seekers frequent this site for its business news content as well as its career information. As mentioned before, content is critical to keep job seekers coming back. Effective marketing will provide name recognition and attract one-time shoppers, but it is content that will keep them loyal. For some job seekers the job they find at the site is all that is necessary, but I believe an excellent site will have both jobs and content.

RECRUITERS ONLINE NETWORK

With over 8,000 registered recruiters, Recruiters Online Network (RON; www.recruitersonline.com) is the world's largest association of recruiters, executive search firms, employment agencies, and employment professionals. It is a virtual worldwide community of employment firms. You can post your jobs once and reach hundreds of locations, search the resume database, work with other recruiters, and take advantage of cost savings. Their mission statement is to help members (third-party recruiters) become more successful in the placement industry by using the Internet and other technology. Memberships start at under $500 per year, with the option to upgrade to the Best of the Net Membership for $1,500 per year. RON also offers a free thirty-day trial membership so you can try before you buy. If you are willing to network with other recruiters and split fees, this is a site you will definitely want to check out.

JOBOPTIONS (FORMERLY E-SPAN)

JobOptions (formerly E-Span), located at www.joboptions.com, offers extensive services—a resume database called HR Tools (offering HR advice and information), automated job posting, Job Alert, and Resume Alert. These last two cool features are similar to e-mail agents on other sites. Job Alert notifies candidates about a close match between the candidate and a job. Resume Alert notifies recruiters of a close match between the job and particular candidates. JobOptions is among the top ten recruitment sites, I believe, because of its superior content for job seekers as well as human resource people. Some of the best-of-class tools the site offers can help job seekers create online resumes quickly in three different styles and formats (online, print, and e-mail)—easily changeable with the click of a button. JobOptions also provides career articles and other up-to-date information regarding salaries, managing careers, and hot new trends in careers. It's no surprise it has nearly 90,000 online resumes.

Chart 9 lists the top ten online job sites as of June 1999 according to *Fortune* magazine. You probably noticed this chart contains some of the same sites ranked in the top ten by IBN, such as Monster.com, CareerMosaic, and Headhunter. Jobsearch is affiliated with Headhunter, and you will be automatically linked to Headhunter when you visit this web site. You have already been introduced to Nationjob and Careerpath, but to refresh your memory, Nationjob uses the push method extremely well. It pushes jobs to job seekers via e-mail and has over 350,000 subscribers.

CHART 9	FORTUNE'S TOP TEN RECRUITMENT WEB SITES	
1. Monster.com	6. Nationjob	
2. Careerpath	7. HotJobs	
3. CareerMosaic	8. Net-Temps*	
4. Jobsearch	9. Dice	
5. Headhunter*	10. CareerBuilder	

*Discussed in Chapter 5
Source: Media Metrix: Fortune, *June 1999*

Careerpath is the national job site affiliated with all the major metropolitan newspapers. The sites listed in Chart 8 that haven't been discussed yet are Nationjob, HotJobs, Dice, and CareerBuilder. More information on these top sites is provided below.

NATIONJOB

Nationjob (www.nationjob.com) is a computerized recruitment service company based in Des Moines, Iowa. It has been providing a computerized job listing service since 1988. Its individual job postings are competitively priced (under $100 per job posting), and it also has several packages to choose from including corporate packages that allow you unlimited postings for a budget price per month or year. The company also offers banner advertising and mini web sites and, of course, links to your own home page.

One of Nationjob's most recognized features is the P.J. Scout. Job seekers just tell the scout what jobs and key words they're searching for, and from then on this free service automatically sends them any new jobs that match their choices via e-mail. Job seekers get a great service, and employers get each job listing promoted across the P.J. Scout subscriber base as well as on the Internet and Nationjob's stand-alone sites. As of January 2000, P.J. was scouting for over 450,000 people every week. Nationjob is also known for its specialty pages, which function as separate web sites to promote clients' jobs to as many people as possible. Each page lists all appropriate openings as well as the logos of featured employers, and attracts additional job seekers via links throughout the Internet. This site has been around a long time, and I expect it to be around a lot longer. The long, distinguished list of employers currently using this site is proof of its valued services.

HOTJOBS

HotJobs (www.hotjobs.com) is just what its name implies—hot. Member companies such as Sun Microsystems and Oracle (just to mention a couple of big names) can search the "hot shots" resume database full of IT job seekers. The member subscription isn't cheap—at last check the annual cost was around $6,000, which includes full access to the resume database and posting twenty jobs. The unique feature of this site is its guarantee policy, which says something like if you haven't made a hire in the first six months HotJobs will refund your money. With guaranteed results like this, why not give it a try? I recently heard HotJobs is branching out to other disciplines such as marketing, sales, and accounting—offered with similar features and services.

DICE

Dice (www.dice.com) is a job search web site for computer professionals. It lists thousands of high-tech permanent, contract, and consulting jobs nationwide for programmers, software engineers, systems administrators, web developers, hardware engineers, and others. Dice allows you to place unlimited job postings for a fair price. New features and time-saving tools are being added all the time. These days Dice is being ranked in most surveys' top ten recruiting sites. Most West Coast recruiters are well aware of it. According to Hitbox statistics, this site is consistently ranked in the top 100 (usually in the top 10) for the number of hits (page views) it is receiving. I believe the people at Hitbox are accurately tracking hits and have a valuable, unbiased service.

CAREERBUILDER

CareerBuilder (www.careerbuilder.com) is the world's largest recruiting network, combining over twenty-five leading career sites, including USA Today, NBC, CNET, and Business Week Online. This combined network reaches a large audience on the web—86 million monthly. It has helped companies such as Microsoft, Oracle, Salomon Smith Barney, and others build a successful recruiting strategy online.

The Best Cyber Hangouts for Finding Information Technology Candidates

Now that you're somewhat familiar with the leading mega sites, you might want to know about leading niche sites. In Appendix C you will find a directory of specialty and niche recruiting web sites. It gives the web site names and web addresses for sites designed for IT candidates,

MBAs and recent graduates, finance/accounting candidates, healthcare professionals, diverse candidates, and engineers/designers. The chart doesn't list these niche sites in any particular order or ranking.

Some niche sites cater just to information technology candidates. Some of the job banks listed in the top ten charts are also super places to find IT candidates even though they aren't listed again in the IT niche site chart. Below are some brief summaries of leading web sites especially for IT candidates.

DEVELOPERS NET COMMUNITY

Increasing competition for the best software developers demands recruiting efforts that are more efficient and cost-effective than headhunting services and classified ads. Developers Net (www.developers.net) effectively interacts with members of the software development community. Because Developers Net is more than a database, it reaches active and passive job seekers who have web, Windows, DBMS, Java, and Unix development expertise. Developers Net members respond individually to job postings with current resumes. Thanks to this comprehensive and convenient source for job and industry information, the online community of over 24,000 software professionals is constantly growing. Microsoft is looking for talent on this site and has a nice little banner blinking here.

COMPUTER JOBS STORE

Computer Jobs Store (www.computerjobs.com) is growing fast. As of January 2000, it had more than 31,000 jobs posted from over 700 companies and offered free postings to its site. Currently targeting some twenty major markets in the United States, by allowing free job postings it hopes to expand to other geographic areas of the country. I expect to see this site catapult to the top of the recruitment lists very quickly.

C++ JOBS DOT COM

For finding C++ and other programmers, C++ Jobs Dot Com (www.cplusplusjobs.com) is worth checking out. You can receive one free seven-day job listing on each of its web sites, which target professionals who are proficient in Lotus Notes, PowerBuilder, and Visual Basic, and other computer professionals. When your listing expires, the site will let you know how many times it was viewed. You may then decide to extend your ad for around $25 for one thirty-day listing or $50 for three thirty-day listings.

CLASSIFIEDS2000

Classifieds2000 (www.classifieds2000.com) is just what its name implies — a high-traffic classifieds site with a separate classification for employment. As of January 2000, it had more than 310,000 jobs posted. Classifieds sites are popping up all over the Internet, as e-commerce is becoming a booming business. People are starting to trust buying things online and are worrying less about sending their credit card information over the information superhighway. Classifieds2000 leads the pack and has teamed up with various radio stations, Internet search engines, and a host of other affiliated sites. Like Yahoo Classifieds, this site attracts passive job seekers looking for a new car, a new computer, or just about anything else.

Classifieds2000 provides complete classifieds service to a network of over 100 leading web sites. Due to its popularity and marketing, many companies are experiencing success with posting their job openings to this site. This site doesn't just offer general employment — I was doing an online job search the other day and found over 100 jobs listed on Classifieds2000 with the key word C++. Some of the companies posting jobs on this site for their computer-related openings were AT&T, Kelly Technical, Manpower Technical, Clarion Solutions, IT Force, CDI Information & Technical, and CTG.

COMPUTER PROFESSIONALS

Computer Professionals (www.ohw.com) is America's online help-wanted site for computer jobs. Computer professionals looking for a new employment challenge search this database, and recruiters looking for the right people for computer-related positions post job openings here. Computer Professionals is concentrated mostly on the East Coast, serving cities such as Raleigh, Boston, Washington, D.C., Charlotte, and Tampa. It also services Los Angeles, Denver, and Chicago.

PROGRAMMING JOBS

Programming Jobs (www.prgjobs.com) is a niche site that is growing daily. It boasts visits upward of 600 programmers each day and over 30,000 resumes in its resume bank. Recruiters also are able to try a free thirty-day trial membership.

JOBS4IT

Jobs4IT (www.jobs4it.com) strictly targets information technology professionals. The service is free to the job seeker and competitively priced with other IT sites for recruiters. I'm not sure how long this site has been in existence, but it seems to be doing a fair job of maximizing its exposure and offering the push technology that both recruiters and job seekers seem to like.

INFOWORKS USA

Infoworks USA (www.it123.com) offers companies a low-cost, effective means of locating top-notch IT candidates. Subscribing clients have the benefits of a comprehensive search process, which greatly enhances their chances of finding the right technical job. This team of professionals promises to take the time to go the "extra mile."

PASSPORTACCESS

PassportAccess (www.passportaccess.com) is a superior site for technical talent. Not long ago, it entered into an agreement with Yahoo and AltaVista that will allow all job postings from PassportAccess to be included in Yahoo Classifieds and AltaVista's new CareerZone. This alliance provides higher visibility to recruiters posting positions on PassportAccess and helps Yahoo and AltaVista continue their expansion into the employment arena. Yahoo and AltaVista combined receive over 200 million page views per day.

PLACEUM 2000

Placeum 2000 (www.placeumit.com) is dedicated to maintaining a solid recruiting environment with information technology professionals. Dealing exclusively with resumes from this population ensures the IT recruiter that resumes found in this database will be only IT candidates. The site reviews all resumes to verify at least one year of IT/IS experience. You can also search for IT candidates by state. A free trial period is available prior to signing up for membership.

COMPUTERWORK

Computerwork (www.computerwork.com) matches computer-job seekers and their skills to computer jobs available through the nation's best recruiting firms. As of January 2000, the site's resume bank provided access to more than 75,000 prequalified experienced IT professionals. Job seekers have told me they've received calls within twenty-four hours after posting their resume to Computerwork. Job seekers also like the feature that notifies them when new positions that match their interest hit the site. Computerwork offers recruiters a free thirty-day trial before signing up.

ZDNET JOB ENGINE

This site (www.jobengine.com) targets information technology professionals via the massive advertising power of Ziff-Davis. Ziff-Davis print publications inform millions of computer professionals that Job Engine is the place to look for career opportunities. Because of this extreme targeted marketing campaign directed toward IT professionals, this site generates high traffic and highly qualified candidates.

Noteworthy Human Resource Niche Sites

I'm a strong proponent of niche sites. I would like to see niche sites focusing more on smaller (regional or community) geographic locations. One of the most common complaints, from recruiters and job seekers alike, is about having to weed through all the out-of-town jobs. Most sites can narrow searching to states, but very few have advanced capabilities to narrow the search even further to specific cities within the state. Hopefully, this little nuisance will disappear as we continue to forge ahead and refine online capabilities.

Again I refer you to the directory of specialty and niche recruiting web sites in Appendix C for names and web addresses of sites for MBAs, finance, healthcare, engineering, and other professional specialties. Below are descriptions of some noteworthy human resource sites.

SOCIETY FOR HUMAN RESOURCE MANAGEMENT (SHRM)

On the top of my list of noteworthy HR niche sites is the Society for Human Resource Management (SHRM; www.shrm.org). It has been the leading meeting place for HR professionals to network, learn, and share information pertinent to this industry. I'm assuming most people reading this book either are members of SHRM or have at least heard of this organization. Founded in 1948, this wonderful organization provides education, information, HR-related conferences and seminars, publications, and online services. This is a site you will definitely want to bookmark.

JOBS4HR

Since the majority of the people reading this book are in the field of human resources, I want to mention a great site located at www.jobs4hr.com. This is a recruiting site targeted for HR positions. The database is filled with several thousand registered job seekers. Your jobs are posted online and e-mailed to qualified candidates who registered via their personal career agent. The service has been completely automated and the online jobs database is now active. In addition, if you want to keep your feelers out for new HR opportunities, all you have to do is sign up for this personal career agent and sit back and wait. Jobs4HR has a simple goal—to find the right match for human resource professionals.

HRWORLD

HR World (www.hrworld.com) is another niche site dedicated to the human resource profession. Positions are posted for various levels and broken out by discipline. Useful information written by various columnists regarding topics of particular interest to HR professionals is also located at this site.

More Noteworthy Sites

I'd like to introduce a couple more sites worth describing in a little greater detail. These sites are also listed in the directory of recruiting web sites in Appendix C.

BEST JOBS USA

This superior site, located at www.bestjobsusa.com, posts employment ads from the *USA Today* newspaper. This site has a free resume depository as well as career events, a career store, and much more.

CAREER MART

Career Mart (www.careermart.com) formed a partnership with AltaVista (which you already know is in the top ten). It offers everything you could possibly want from a recruitment site—a superior resume bank, chat rooms, career advice, and e-mail agents (a hot item for both job seekers and recruiters). It also has a long list of well-known corporate clients.

Where Do I Post?

Now that you know strategies of online recruiting and some top cyber hangouts for the industries in which you are recruiting, you need to decide whether you want to post to a job board, your corporate web site, Usenets, or a combination of any or all of these.

If you are new to online recruiting, you may be wondering what your competition and other leading companies around the world are doing. According to IBN, most job postings (61 percent) have been placed on Usenets, 33 percent on job boards, and the remaining 6 percent on corporate web sites. You may be asking yourself, should I be posting to Usenets instead of my job board? Usenets, you may remember, are user networks of people with special interests in common. They were one of the first places for job seekers to hear about job opportunities. As I mentioned in Chapter 5, many Usenets are stopping free posting to their newsgroups.

So, I believe the utility of Usenets as an avenue for postings will soon diminish, while corporate and individual web sites will experience an increase in job postings. As creating corporate web sites (even for small businesses) has become easier, more companies are moving toward placing all their job postings on their own corporate site, with banners on major commercial portals to drive job seekers to their site.

FAST FACTS

Where Are the Jobs Posted?

61% on Usenets
33% on job boards

Source: IBN: interbiznet.com 1999 Electronic Recruiting Index Executive Summary

This strategy seems to work fairly well because it involves more Internet exposure. Diversification works as well for online recruiting as it does for managing stocks. Find out what works best for you and your unique situation and get as much online exposure as possible. Creative recruitment advertisements and job postings to lure even the most content job seekers, combined with strategic placement of those postings or banners on high-traffic sites, will increase your rate of success.

Following are ten questions to ask when selecting a recruitment web site.

1. How current are your job listings and how long do you keep listings in your database?
2. How do you handle expiration dates?
3. Do you target specific job seekers or industries?
4. What are the demographics of the job seekers you want to attract?
5. Do you offer career or job-related links for job seekers?
6. Do you charge the job seeker for any services?
7. How do you obtain resumes? From Usenets or other job sites? How current are they? Can job seekers post their resumes confidentially?
8. Do you have any method of tracking responses or page views of your job listings? How many visitors do you receive?
9. How many other search engines and sites do you advertise on to attract candidates?
10. How long have you been providing this service? Can I speak to a customer who is using your services now?

Conclusion

In 1998, consumer research indicated there were more computer monitors purchased than televisions and more e-mails received than telephone calls. And that was just the beginning. Personal computers have become so user-friendly and affordable, even seniors are rushing out to purchase these machines. I never thought I would see the day I would be receiving electronic mail from my mother, but I do on a daily basis. As time goes on, I believe the computer will become as common as the television in our households. The Internet is here to stay. Fiber-optic cables are likely to replace modem lines, but Internet use will continue to grow to infinite proportions. The paradigm shift has altered recruitment forever. The amount of information on the Internet is enormous, but we can access it if we have a map and some help to point us in the right direction.

KEY CONCEPTS

>> When choosing a web site, review industry surveys such as IBN's Electronic Recruiting Index Survey or Media Metrix to see what others are saying. These surveys will help you make better recruitment decisions.

>> If you are recruiting in a specific field, such as information technology, human resources, or another specialty field, use niche sites or job boards specifically targeting your job category. For example, if you are hiring mostly computer professionals, a great niche site would be Computer Jobs Store (www.computerjobs.com).

>> Usenets used to be the number one place job seekers and recruiters online could find one another. They are still popular places to post jobs, but more and more companies are moving toward posting their jobs to major commercial sites. Most companies have their own corporate web site and are also purchasing banners on major commercial portals to drive job seekers to their web site.

Chapter Seven

Forecast for the Future of Online Recruiting

My forecast is the sky is the limit. The Internet has been around for a while, but only recently has it become hugely successful—probably due to the decreasing cost of computers and increasingly easy access to the web, and maybe the invention of Java, the language of the web. Except for research and sharing information, until recently the Internet was not a standard part of our daily life. The words *World Wide Web* would have been unfamiliar to the average person less than a decade ago. But that was before the Internet revolutionized the way we conduct business. Today's educational institutions will have to start offering courses in e-commerce, and our future MBAs will need to know a lot about the power of the Internet to survive in this new business environment. For those who had hoped the Internet and online recruiting were just a fad that would go away as quickly as they arrived, I'm sorry for this bit of bad news. They're here to stay and will continue to become more instrumental in the human resource trade. Experts agree that the World Wide Web is one of the most successful marketing avenues of the last century and recruiting on the Internet is one of the leaders of the pack.

If you don't believe me, consider the following statistics.

FAST FACTS

>> 65 % of U.S. public schools were connected to the Internet in 1996. The president's initiative to connect all of the nation's public schools to the Internet by 2003 is right on schedule. As of December 1999, 85% of schools were connected to the Internet. Of those, 58% had access from at least one classroom, 54% from a computer lab, and 70% from a library/media center.

Source: U.S. Department of Education

>> 48 % of employers think the web has raised productivity.

Source: The Society for Human Resource Management

>> 20 million Americans consider the Internet indispensable.

Source: SourceFind/SVP 1997 American Internet User Survey

>> According to Forrester Research reports, there were over 6,500 job sites on the Internet in 1998 compared to only 500 job sites in 1995. Online recruiting expenditures were expected to increase from 30 million in 1998 to over 200 million in 2000.

Cost Savings

You would think the cost of Internet recruiting would be on a spiral downward; however, when demand is up, cost goes up. Hopefully, in the future, the cost of Internet recruiting will be driven down by increased competition and more efficient ways of doing business. The cost savings may have to be valued in the cost per hire rather than the cost to post or recruit online. For example, iLogos Corporation, a research and consulting company specializing in Internet recruiting, announced that in 1998 more than three-quarters of the companies surveyed reported cost savings from implementing an Internet recruiting program. One Fortune 500 computer manufacturer surveyed by iLogos indicated the per-employee recruitment costs shown at left.

FAST FACTS

Per-Employee Recruitment Costs

Headhunter	$12,500
Newspaper ad.	$ 5,000
Job fair	$ 3,000
Campus recruiting	$ 2,000
Internet	$ 1,000

Source: iLogos Corporation

According to a report from the Saratoga Institute, an HR research organization, in 1998 it took companies an average of fifty-nine days to fill an open position. This translated into costs of over $60,000 from the work not being performed in each open position. That equates to a loss of over $1,000 per day from the lack of a trained, productive employee contributing to a company's bottom line. These figures do not take into account other direct costs of hiring, such as agency fees and print advertising. According to Saratoga Institute, U.S. companies spent $8,512 on average in direct costs to hire one exempt employee in 1998. In more specialized disciplines this cost was even higher.

FAST FACTS

>> 59+ days on average to fill an open position

>> $60,000 in costs from work not being performed

>> $8,512 average direct costs to hire one exempt employee

>> $2,620 average cost of a newspaper ad

Source: Saratoga Institute 1998 research report

In the iLogos study, the average cost of a successful newspaper ad was $2,620. Compare this with a similar posting on the Internet for less than $100 (or for free on some sites).

Who Will Survive the Shakeout?

Job sites seem to be growing at exponential rates, and if you're waiting for the growth trend to peak, you will have a long wait. The peak seems to be nowhere in sight. Even with the growth rate, online recruiting still represents only a small percentage of ad dollars spent on recruiting. The majority of advertising dollars is still devoted to traditional print media. So if the newspaper giants are wondering where they fit in, it looks as if they still have a good deal of the market share of recruitment advertising dollars.

In the twenty-first century, Internet recruiting will continue offering more customized services for job seekers and recruiters. I expect in the end only the players who have been innovative and successful in anticipating change will survive. While career-related sites are predicted to continue to grow at rapid rates, I believe the niche sites will rise to the top. The Internet has crowded, confusing sites overloaded with information the average job seeker doesn't care about. Specialty sites geared toward a specific discipline, expertise, industry, or geographic area, which may have been zapped out by the big players, will return to prominence. The niche sites will evolve into just a few major sites.

I see community hubs evolving as an extension of these niche sites. For example, every major city will have a major employment community hub. Major sites such as CareerMosaic and Monster.com may power the hub, but the end users will never know what is running in the background. They won't care, either. They'll be able to find a home, a job, a vet, a dentist, and a doctor. They will learn about school districts in their community with the click of a button. A local site doing this in Rochester, New York, is called Smart Dog. This site advertises in places like California's billboards, trying to catch the eye of a frustrated high-tech motorist tired of a two-hour commute to work. Smart Dog partners with over 1,700 companies in and around Rochester. Job seekers in California or anywhere can visit this site and learn anything they want about companies in Rochester—as well as about the lifestyle, churches, schools, and activities of interest to them.

One great source for finding such community hubs is Real Cities (www.realcities.com), a national network of regional portals featuring local information sites in thirty U.S. cities. Unlike national networks and stand-alone web sites, Real Cities hubs specialize in providing extensive local information. The focus and goal are to provide a variety of choices and a wide array of information in a single location on the web so users don't have to hop around the Internet to find the information they need. Users also have the option to search the entire web if they choose. Each city guide contains an in-depth directory of information and services searchable by category.

Hot New Trends

Technology is growing by the millisecond—we may as well embrace it. The first step toward embracing new technology is to learn how it can help you fill your job orders. Isn't that the point of technology—to help you fill your open requisitions with the most suitable candidates available in the least amount of time? When I first started researching online recruiting, I thought I would need to go back to college for a degree in computer science in order to understand the technical terminology. If you're like most recruiters, you probably had never heard of web spiders or robots (before you read Chapter 4) and didn't have a clue what they could do to help you find candidates. Let me assure you, I didn't have to study computer science in college to understand and speak the language of the Internet. You don't have to know how the carburetor works to drive a car. It's the same with Internet recruiting. Don't even try to figure out the technology—just concentrate on learning how to put the car in drive to get you where you want to go. However, if you would like advanced training, there are a number of companies that offer advanced Internet recruiting strategies and seminars. One that comes to mind is Advanced Internet Recruitment Strategies (AIRS). AIRS doesn't teach you how or where to post your job openings or what resume banks to search—it teaches strategies to help you find passive candidates, not job seekers. It has tracked down candidates all over the globe and checked all the nooks and crannies of online communities. AIRS focuses on passive candidates who are content at work and hidden deep inside databases, archives, and directories.

VIDEO INTERVIEWING

I predict video interviewing will become more common in the near future. This technology has evolved out of pure necessity. The Internet has extended our reach for potential candidates to the entire globe. This is a good thing, but it causes some logistical problems, such as interviewing when there are 5,000 miles between candidates and employers. Several types of video interviewing technology are available. Microsoft's NetMeeting® was introduced not too long ago and is available for free through a download option at Microsoft's web site. You also have Intel, 8x8, AT&T, Eastman Kodak, and a host of other companies offering video telephone equipment for under $1,000. This technology is still trying to find a place in the online recruiting world. Even though it is fairly easy to use, video technology isn't extensively used yet. I believe sometime in the near future, as the bugs get worked out (and the pictures stop looking as if they are coming from Mars), we will see wider acceptance.

ISDN (integrated services digital network) videoconferencing is also available. It offers high-speed connection at a higher price, and, of course, the quality is much better. Kinko's offers videoconferencing services for rent by the hour in most of its branch offices in most major cities. If you're responsible for coordinating hiring for an office, I recommend you look into this technology. The money you save on one candidate's airfare pays for the equipment. My feeling is, if you fly more than five candidates per year to interview with your company, you can benefit from video interviewing. Companies save money and candidates save time. They don't have to take time off to make the trip. Remember, the person you want for the job is most likely already working and will be more willing to interview via videophone than to make a personal trip to the company.

Setting up the video call is as easy as making a telephone call. The videophone is similar to the fax machine. The sender and the receiver each need the equipment. I purchased two videophones—one for me and one to ship to the candidate. I can have the equipment shipped overnight and picked up the next day by courier. All the candidate has to do is plug it into his or her phone and wait for my call. Eventually a product like Microsoft NetMeeting, with camera and sound, will be a standard feature on desktops. Just think what this technology can do for the entertainment industry—live singing and dancing auditions over the Internet!

MORE SIT-BACK-AND-WAIT OPTIONS IN THE FUTURE

We need to find more ways to perfect the sit-back-and-wait approach so we have more time for our families, friends, customers, and job seekers, and to enjoy life. I predict job seekers will demand more tools to help them find jobs more effortlessly. This is the wave of future successful online recruiting. It has evolved out of necessity because more job seekers are employed and don't have the time to search through thousands of jobs on the Internet. They are using more automatic e-mail notification agents. Bridgepath (located at www.bridgepath.com) designed a service that specifically matches the interest of the job seeker with job postings hitting its site. This trend toward letting the job find the candidate is going to be a standard offering on major sites that want to stay competitive in the future. Nationjob (www.nationjob.com) also offers a superior automatic e-mail-notifying agent called the P.J. Scout. I expect these cool automatic notification tools will become the standard on leading career sites.

WANTED JOBS 98

Wanted Technologies is a Quebec-based company launched in 1997 that develops solutions to efficiently manage the mountains of employment information available on the Internet. The company's first product, Wanted Jobs 98, is a free job search management tool that has received accolades from some top software reviewers. Since January of 1999 I have frequently used this free downloaded software in two ways: (1) for searching online jobs for my clients and (2) for keeping up to date on Internet job sites. This handy tool also helps me keep track of who's leading the pack in job postings for particular disciplines such as information technology and engineering. For example, when I run a search under the key word *engineering*, this software goes to the leading job banks (America's Job Bank, Nationjob, CareerCity, CareerMosaic, to mention just a few) and provides a report of jobs it found meeting my criteria, how many were found, and on which sites. In my opinion, this type of software is exactly what online recruiting is all about—helping the job seeker find the jobs. How long do you think recruiting on the Internet will remain popular if the growing number of job posting sites becomes so unmanageable that just the thought of doing an online job search is horrifying to the average job seeker? Hats off to innovative companies such as Wanted Technologies for inventing a useful tool to help job seekers and recruiting professionals increase their ease of searching online jobs.

ONLINE COMMUNITIES

Look for more online communities evolving on the web. One company doing an excellent job of building valuable online communities is Tapestry. This company has been targeting IT professionals and bilingual candidates from Developers Net and ITinfo (which has a bilingual job site). You can expect to receive resumes within seventy-two hours for each job that you broadcast. All the resumes are from professionals in your recruiting area interested in working for your company. Niche and targeted online communities will become more popular. You will see more Internet users logging onto specific sites that have the information they are looking for without searching around. Web designers need to build content-rich environments to create a loyal community of users.

The downside of Internet recruiting is for the job seekers. They are going to be given such an overwhelming array of job sites, career advice sites, and online job pitches that they will be more confused than ever. This creates the need for such wonderful books as *CareerXRoads* (www.careerxroads.com) by Gerry Crispin and Mark Mehler. This is a directory of the best sites on the web for resume and career management with reviews, techniques, and advice for job seekers. The authors also offer a free mailing service for monthly updates to their directory.

DRIVE TO USE THE NETWORK

The drive to automate is here to stay. I see a trend toward using the network for most business applications (not just Internet recruiting). This may be because my husband, Ron, has been employed with Sun Microsystems since 1996. Back then, the Internet was just flickering into prominence. Sun Microsystems saw its potential almost a decade ago, embraced its technology, and invented web computing and application software products such as Java. I used to wear a T- shirt with a big cup of coffee and the Java logo across the front and back. People used to ask me where they could buy Sun Java coffee. Now when I wear the shirt, people say things such as "I love using Java, it is so easy" and "Do you work for Sun Microsystems?" It's amazing to me how, in such a short period, Java has spread all over the Internet and become a standard course taught at colleges and universities. How did Java brew so quickly when it took ten years for C++ to be offered at the university level? Java is the programming language of choice on the web. Programmers have adopted it widely and most web sites have Java running in the background.

Another point I would like to make here is that Sun has been operating just fine without the use of Windows or PCs. The company is one of the forerunners in performing all its business functions over its network. I foresee the switch to the network happening rapidly over the next few years. Companies will demand one combined smart card to plug in to operate recruiting, hiring, payroll, office tasks, and all areas of their business. Look for one platform to deliver information, phone, video, e-mail, fax, automated scheduling. All our daily needs will be met through the computer network and will be automated, and the information we access will be in digital form. We are very close to this now at the dawn of the new millennium.

GROWTH OF E-COMMERCE

Dell Computer Corporation announced its intention to increase its e-commerce to more than 50 percent of its business by the year 2000 (Gates, 1999). Dell is not the only company looking to increase its online business. Expect to see more and more online ads driving people to shop for jobs, merchandise, and services online.

More Future Net Trends

Can you imagine a recruiter or any company communicating more with computer networks than with the telephone? This is the trend of communication in the future. We will rely more on computers, video technology, and the Internet as our main communication media. Many entrepreneurs are perfecting gadgets this very minute to deliver a product that will allow us to throw out our telephones. Thirty years ago, would you have believed the typewriter would be an obsolete item in the office environment? Well, thirty years from now the standard phone will more than likely be used only to hook up our mainframe computer or Internet connection.

Also expect to see the paper resume become nearly extinct. With almost every major site offering an online submission form for job openings, and with e-mail as the preferred method of communication, online resume transmission will far exceed traditional "snail mail" delivery in the future. The paper resume may still come in handy for networking with friends and colleagues in person; however, sending resumes via nontraditional methods (fax, e-mail, and online delivery) is more efficient and cost-effective. So requests such as "e-mail me your resume and I'll forward it to the right person" are becoming more common, while the paper resume is starting to collect dust on the corner of your desk, waiting to be put in an envelope and snail mailed.

The demand of parents to work from home is increasing, and with 50 percent of U.S. households predicted to be interconnected by the new millennium we should have more people wired and working from home. Could it be possible that in the future most of us will have the option to work from home and meet clients and co-workers online via video and audio hardware? I see this happening in the not-too-distant future. Look at how far we've come in just the last quarter-century.

One-Stop Career Centers and Workforce Initiatives

Another trend I see is government-funded one-stop career centers. They are already functioning successfully in Massachusetts (at www.masscareers.state.ma.us) and Virginia. Implementation and development grants are under way in most major cities, and by the time this book is in print, most of them will be up and running. The United States government has devoted a substantial heap of grant money to establish the workforce development system. The old workforce training system consisted of fragmented and wasteful programs. The Department of Labor had one intake process for qualifying job seekers, and other agencies, such as the Departments of Human Services, Education, Job Training, and others, had completely different intake processes and structures. Job seekers would have to apply at each individual office to determine eligibility. The one-stop career centers are going to streamline all the agencies to link together to share information. The result will be a "no wrong door policy." If job seekers go to the wrong agency for benefits, they will still be processed and referred appropriately, regardless of their entry point. This new way of doing business in federal, state, and local agencies will change the way private sector employers find employees, too. I believe that America's Job Bank (which is funded through the U.S. Department of Labor) will become even more popular and will play a critical role in helping employers and job seekers find one another. As the one-stop career centers become more accessible, more employers and job seekers will use them.

I would keep track of what is happening in your city regarding one-stop career centers. A survey of 200 Massachusetts business managers showed that 82 percent would be likely to use one of these new centers. By contrast, only 3 percent said they were likely to use any of the employment programs currently offered by public agencies in Massachusetts. I sincerely believe that U.S. government agencies will become more strategic partners in our recruiting efforts in the very near future. They are becoming more technologically advanced to accommodate our needs. They currently have, in my opinion, one of the premier job sites available. I hope using America's Job Bank and the one-stop career centers will soon become a standard business practice. It would be a waste of our tax dollars if we didn't take full advantage of these services offered to us by Uncle Sam.

Three Steps Forward and Four Steps Back

I believe we have made many strides in the online recruitment area, yet at the same time, we have gone backwards. At the beginning of the Internet explosion there were just a handful of job sites available. As of January 2000, there were somewhere around 25,000 fee-based job sites operating on the Internet. Some experts estimate there are more than 200,000 job-related Internet sites online. When you take into account all the companies that are posting job openings on their web sites, you can understand why the numbers are so high. I believe we have reached a saturation point with the Internet and online recruitment. The existence of too many sites has hurt us—we've reached a point of diminishing returns. In the future I see online recruitment going back to a more community-based approach with regional and niche focuses. I hope that the leading national sites come up with a way to accomplish this—to join as partners rather than competitors. Wouldn't you like to have access to every job seeker looking for work through one resume bank? Wouldn't you like to know you could enter your jobs into one job bank and be assured that every job seeker in your geographic area and discipline would have access to it? Maybe someday the government-sponsored site America's Job Bank or some other large commercial site will be that place.

Who Will Be the Survivors?

Is all this technology replacing good old recruiting methods? Do we already spend more time interacting with technology than with live human beings? I know I spend more time with my computer than I'd like to. I have more e-mail conversations and online chats than I do telephone conversations. And when I do use the telephone, I talk more to voice messaging machines than to real live folks. (When I want to speak with a customer service rep and I get a ten-minute voice mail recording, I just press zero and usually get connected with a human being. Just thought I'd pass this little trick on to you in case you haven't figured it out yet.) Since we've already invested quite heavily in technology, we must embrace it openly. We can use the little tricks from Chapter 4 or press zero when we absolutely must speak to a live human being. In order to keep our sanity, the trick is to create a balance. A successful recruiter or job seeker cannot rely on technology alone. Technology must be viewed as a tool or an added-value service—not the entire service. Human beings require human compassion. The golden rule and the old adage "the customer is always right" still must stand paramount to technology. Sometimes they get buried beneath all the technology.

I know a human resource manager for a fairly large company who absolutely refuses to answer his phone, even if he is sitting at his desk filing his fingernails. He believes he's managing his time well by screening his calls and only responding to callers he chooses to talk to. Is this a balance of technology? Well, you could say this management practice has been going on since the invention of the telephone—instead of voice mail, a secretary screened the calls. That may be true, but this same manager uses e-mail 90 percent of the time when he should be talking to an employee about an uncomfortable subject. How is technology affecting the way we are interacting with people? Are we sending out e-mails to avoid personal confrontation? It is important to find the balance between technology and human interaction.

WHERE DOES THE EXECUTIVE SEARCH FIRM FIT IN?

Will companies want to pay hefty placement fees in the future? Will they still pay for retained searches? Yes and no. I believe headhunters, contingency placement firms, electronic research bureaus, and executive search firms will all survive—but only those that are flexible, innovative, and extremely client focused. More than ever, they will need to remain current with recruitment trends and more cost competitive than ever before. They will need to be willing to change their operating structure and services to fit the needs of the clients. They must become expert in online recruiting. I forecast that companies will expect more from headhunters and executive search firms. They may want innovative orientations, pre-screening, drug testing, career pathing, or some other form of training or service to be included with the price tag.

WHERE DOES THE NEWSPAPER INDUSTRY FIT IN?

Did the television replace the radio? Did airplanes replace trains and automobiles? In my opinion, there is always room for different media and each has its own advantages and disadvantages. I believe the push for a paperless society is still futuristic and lacks the personal touch humans enjoy so much. There is something cozy about sitting next to a fireplace in your favorite chair reading a book or a newspaper. You can smell the print, flip the pages quickly or slowly, and highlight something that strikes your fancy and you want to remember. This may be a quirk of a generation that grew up without learning the basics of working with a computer in kindergarten, but I really don't think so. I think even our children's children will still enjoy hard-copy books and the enticement of a headline on a newspaper's front page.

As I mentioned in the Introduction, newspapers have been worried that doomsday may be just around the corner because of the Internet's easy access to information. But at last check, newspapers were still in business and seemed to have come to terms with the online world. Rather than fighting it, they joined forces with it and offered a combination service approach—many metropolitan newspapers have some digital edition of their paper. I believe the power of print is enormous and the Internet hasn't weakened this power to any major extent. The newspaper companies paid attention to the market and changed some of their strategies. For example, it's not uncommon to see a newspaper displaying a full-page ad for a virtual career fair. This sort of advertising is still generating revenue for the newspaper and filling a need for the clients to attract job seekers.

I believe the good news for the newspaper industry is that the Sunday want ads will be around for a long time. The bad news is that revenue will be lost in print recruitment advertising and will have to be regained through other venues (such as online career fairs) to compete with online recruiting. Newspapers will offer career advice online or develop online communities to provide a value-added service for job seekers. The *Washington Post* and many other major newspapers are doing an excellent job of providing free services to job seekers, which keeps them coming back for more. There is a higher cost to print advertising, so it's more cost-effective for newspapers to offer online information and links to other services without taking up column-inch space in the newspaper.

Employee Retention—Now That I've Found Them, How Do I Keep Them?

My passion has been helping people find a career—not just a job—and that's the key to employee retention. This means hiring the right candidate, not only for the right job, but also for the right company. Some people thrive in a small organization and others feel claustrophobic. The personality characteristics of job seekers are hard to assess but critical to successful placement. The Japanese capitalize on this and remain extremely successful in building employee loyalty, which is practically shatterproof. When a premier company hires you, you know you are set for life. You become part of the family and reap all the benefits of the company and the security of lifetime employment. When employees were hired at General Motors, IBM, or Kodak, there used to be a certain loyalty and security that came along with the company badge. The promise of lifetime employment and security is a product of yesterday. It is not unusual to find job seekers changing jobs two or three times a year rather than a lifetime.

With the Japanese, there are many variables to consider, but their culture is not something we can easily duplicate here in the United States. The Deming philosophy has been widely taught around the globe by many companies trying to duplicate the success of Japanese companies with employee loyalty, productivity, and product quality. We didn't duplicate the Japanese lifetime employment philosophy and, in my opinion, we created a business environment that is more hostile and unstable than ever. People are transferred, leave, retire, quit, or are laid off. Many companies going through downsizing find their key employees jumping ship even though they run little risk of being downsized. But in reality they are at risk because during the reorganizing their careers frequently come to a standstill. This is a common occurrence when companies are going through difficult changes. A paradox occurs where one department is laying off employees and the department across the hall is hiring new people. There is very little matching of transferable skills—downsized employees could be retained if companies were willing to invest in retraining instead of recruiting new employees.

Companies that are reorganizing need to look at ways to capitalize on their existing human resource investments. Training and education must be stressed not only to develop employees' careers but also to ensure the survival of the company. Many Japanese companies have perfected the art of strategic planning and have a bank of trained employees ready to bring a product or service to market. We must start looking at the long-term investment in our people and stop cutting ourselves short. Training and development are usually the first areas of a budget to be cut when a company experiences trouble—it should be the first area to improve in times of trouble.

As a recruiting professional, regardless of whether you are the VP of personnel or running a one-person office, it's important to keep the candidate's best interests in mind. You need to ask yourself, is this person really a good fit for the company in the long run? If your candidate has aspirations of becoming a VP of human resources within a few years and you know the company is outsourcing this area of the business, is she or he really the best candidate? How long do you think the candidate will stay with this company once reality has set in? Have you really helped your company or client by ignoring the job seeker's career goals?

Too often, we hire employees and forget about them. I believe new employees should have a career director or mentor assigned to them.

There should be some type of support and feedback mechanism in place. Human resource policies need to be looked at objectively and reassessed continually. What are exit interviews telling us? What are the employees telling us they want? Has your company implemented flexible work hours and vacation banks? If it has, are managers allowing employees to make use of these benefits? A problem I see in companies with high employee turnover is that policies are written in handbooks but are not actually implemented. This causes more morale damage than not having any policies at all. With the labor pool in critically low supply, we must concentrate more on retention, training, and development, and safeguarding our most precious resources, our employees.

Conclusion

The purpose of this chapter was to give you a quick peek at future trends of Internet recruiting. Expect many more gadgets and gizmos to become available. To keep abreast of the new trends and tools, I recommend visiting the Online Staffing Report located at www.sireport.com/articles/online9811.html.

My goal in writing this book was to help the experienced online recruiter, the rookie, and everyone in between improve their Internet recruiting strategies. There are some excellent books on the market showing recruiters where to find the best candidates online. One comes with an accompanying CD listing all the URL addresses. So I didn't focus on the "where to" but rather on the "how to." I also tried to focus on the introduction to all the new tools available to us. I hope I was successful in introducing you to the worldwide Internet recruiting explosion. I hope I provided the tools to get you started or, if you are an experienced practitioner, there were some new concepts to benefit you or your company. You can have an arsenal of tools and firsthand knowledge of every online job bank, but what good will that knowledge be if you don't know how to use it? What good will it do to search a resume database full of candidates with the right qualifications if you're unable to extract their resumes? This would happen if you didn't know the critical importance of using appropriate key words to maximize your results. What good would all this technology be if you didn't know how to handle job seekers tactfully?

My goal was also to introduce you to a wide variety of services and tools to make your online recruiting experience less confusing and more user-friendly. I promise you my intention in introducing services was to help you make decisions to make your job easier. I have no personal alliances or financial obligations to mention any service in this book. Many of the services I may have only heard or read about without firsthand knowledge. I tried hard to discuss only reputable providers with an established customer list and credible track record. The vast array of information on the superhighway seems endless, confusing, and cumbersome. We can't expect to ever catch up and harness it; it is just too huge.

Hopefully, this book not only introduced you to innovative tools for online recruiting but also provided you with the map and directions for driving on the Internet recruiting superhighway. I also hope I gave you enough navigation tools for you to take shortcuts to get to your destinations, follow the right road signs and obey traffic signals, know what to do if you get lost or enter a bad neighborhood, and, most important, enjoy the journey.

The key to successful recruiting online, I believe, is to stay current, stay focused, continuously improve your skills, and experiment with ways of perfecting the process of recruiting, hiring, and retaining employees. I heard a writer describing the Internet explosion the other day. He said if we were travelers starting on a journey around the Internet world and we were starting from San Francisco, we wouldn't have even reached the Golden Gate Bridge yet. I believe we have just begun to comprehend the power of this magnificent communication tool. Our journey is just beginning.

In regard to online recruiting, I believe the "where" is not as important as the "how." How we use the available online resources will determine our success or failure. We are working with software and hardware, but we are also dealing with people. We should be letting the software free us so we have more time to spend with these human beings, whether they are our customers, employees, job seekers, or applicants.

Tony Robbins, the famous personal development guru, has a saying: "The definition of insanity is doing the same thing over and over and expecting something different." Are we doing the same things over and over again—treating employees the same and wondering why they are leaving? Are we writing the same policies, placing the same job postings in the same journals, posting the same job description on the same job site, and expecting different results? Maybe it's time to take a journey into cyberspace and try something new. The results just might surprise you.

KEY CONCEPTS

>> The cost of Internet recruiting will remain the same or possibly increase over the next few years. The demand for innovative recruitment sites will remain high, so you won't see any substantial lowering of costs.

>> Newspapers and other print media will still have a place in the future of recruiting. However, since they have lost some recruitment advertising dollars to online recruitment, they will have to generate new revenue through other avenues, such as advertisements for virtual career fairs, job fairs, and online digital services.

>> Niche sites will rise to the top and become more prevalent in the future. Specialty sites geared toward a specific discipline, expertise, industry, or geographic area will return and be the preference for job seekers and recruiters. Community hubs and online gathering places on the Internet will be the entry point to these niche sites or will evolve from them.

>> Video interviewing and new technology will become more common. Global recruiting will be more commonplace and video interviewing will be the medium to help accomplish hiring for distant locations around the globe.

>> More sit-back-and-wait options will become available. Time will become our most precious commodity. Job seekers will demand more tools to help them find jobs more effortlessly. Automatic e-mail notification tools will become standard on leading career sites.

>> The drive to use the network will increase rapidly over the next few years. Companies will demand one combined smart card to plug into all areas of their business enterprise. One platform will deliver information, phone, video, e-mail, automated scheduling, and more.

>> The growth of e-commerce will expand rapidly across all businesses and services.

>> The paper resume will become nearly extinct. It will be used only for personal net-working. All submissions to employers will be handled via fax, e-mail, and online applications.

>> One-stop career centers and workforce initiatives sponsored by funding from the U.S. government will be up and running in every state in the near future. Expect to tap into a highly skilled and educated employee pool (the new workforce) through these centers.

>> Online recruiting will return to a more community-based approach with regional and niche focuses. A few major sites will evolve and emerge as the leaders in online recruiting.

>> A successful recruiter or job seeker cannot rely on technology alone. Technology is a tool or an added-value service—not the entire service.

>> Executive search firms will still exist in the future. They will have to become experts in online recruiting. They will want to offer innovative services such as orientations, pre-screening, drug testing, career pathing, and even training as part of their service.

>> Hiring the right candidate for the job is the key to employee retention. We must start looking at long-term investments in our people. The job doesn't end when you hand an employee his or her name badge. All new employees should have a career director or mentor assigned to them. All employees should have continuous feedback and a defined career path.

>> The key to successful recruiting online is to stay current, stay focused, continuously improve your skills, and experiment with ways of perfecting the process of recruiting, hiring, and retaining employees.

Getting Started

Getting started with online recruiting is easy, getting addicted is even easier, and once you start, you will probably never turn back. To begin interacting effectively in cyberspace you will need a computer or PC, Internet
access, and an e-mail address. I will not go into much detail regarding commercial service providers or modem connectivity because there are countless books in print regarding these topics and I would rather leave these topics to the computer gurus and systems analysts. I would, however, like to
make one crucial technical recommendation regarding the speed of your
connection. If you plan on using the Internet in your recruiting process to
any extent, it is well worth your investing in a high-speed modem, ISDN
line, or the new super-fast cable Internet provider service. There is nothing
more frustrating than having to wait several minutes every time you perform
a search or query. Modem speed continues to increase. As of this writing the
standard baud rate is 56K, with 128K just around the corner.

Cable is also coming of age and offers the fastest connectivity without
the use of phone lines. I believe the future of Internet connection will be
along cable lines rather than telephone lines. I have been using cable networks rather than phone lines for my Internet access for over a year now.
The service is super fast and can outrun any modem on the market. In seconds you're online, then *click click*, you can be checking e-mail, and click
click, you're downloading files in seconds instead of hours. This is far superior to any other Internet service I've ever used. You never have to worry
about a busy signal or the frustration of waiting to log on. The monthly fee
is only slightly higher than telephone Internet service, but when you consider that you don't have to pay for another phone line (since the service
is provided over cable lines), the price works out to be similar to the cost
of noncable Internet service—and it's faster. Consumers are starting to
consider instantaneous information a requirement rather than a luxury. If
you decide to outsource your Internet recruiting activities, these items are
not required, but they are highly recommended.

Having a separate e-mail address to handle incoming resumes and inquiries is also critical. In my opinion, every recruiter and HR professional should have a dedicated e-mail address just for handling incoming resumes. I once made the mistake of using my personal e-mail address for incoming resumes. Before I knew it, I was misplacing resumes every time I opened my mailbox because they were getting mixed up with my personal mail. In order to track the resumes effectively, it is best to have them all come into one central location and be logged immediately upon receipt. If you haven't been involved in the electronic resume process yet, you will soon see that large quantities of resumes start coming in very quickly. If you are with a small company, you may want to think about assigning one person the task of handling electronic resumes. By just doing this, you streamline one step of the recruiting process and lessen the possibility of misplacing a resume, or being unable to verify receipt when you get a call from a candidate, or being unsure if you forwarded it to the appropriate person. This process will eliminate some of the confusion.

I would also like to caution you about printing too much. You know you're printing too much if you're always running out of toner or paper, your file drawers are overflowing, and you have difficulty finding documents in the mountains of paper piled up all over the place. The beauty of Internet recruiting is the paperless society it permits to those who welcome it. I found myself printing every e-mail note I received until I realized I could electronically file things so I could find them later. You can set up e-mail folders. Ask someone familiar with e-mail to show you how. It's really quite simple and serves as a very useful tool in online recruiting. For example, you can set up a mailbox folder titled "Dept. 31" or "DBA Specialists." You just click and drag the e-mailed resumes to the appropriate mailbox folder. This makes them accessible for forwarding to a manager or reviewing at a later date. It is very important to maintain your own internal tracking system or invest in resume tracking and maintenance storage systems. Reactive rather than proactive thinking will be a huge mistake—proper planning is the main ingredient in human resource management for the future. The online world is dynamic—by the time you read this book some of the information may already be outdated.

The Internet is over twenty-five years old and was started by our protective brothers in the U.S. Department of Defense. The Defense Department Advanced Research Projects Agency (ARPA) needed a system to link research teams with computer centers around the world. Access to the general public was denied and only the military, defense contractors, and research universities had access to the information. This Internet was quite different from the commercial entity it is now. The concept of interconnection and the mission are still the same—to share information globally and to link researchers (and now the public) to instant information. As a human resource professional you can enjoy the benefits of instantly expanding your recruiting efforts around the globe. You can also enjoy instant access to HR-related topics, discussions, law, trends, and networking with other colleagues. If you're not already hooked, you will be soon.

Frequently Asked Questions About Online Recruiting

Q: Where should I post my job openings?

A: You may not like my answer to this question, but where you should post your openings depends on where you are located, your company, what job openings you are posting, and a number of other variables. In Chapters 5 and 6, I provide enough information regarding the leading job sites for you to decide the most suitable places to post according to your budget, location, and unique situation. Just remember, the best site isn't worth a dime if your job posting isn't read. The biggest isn't always the best, and what works for another company may not work for your firm. Your company may be in a geographic location that isn't very appealing, and no matter what site you are advertising on, you may not receive the number of qualified candidates you would like to receive. So put your job seeker's shoes on again. What challenging and exciting opportunities can you offer to make it worth my while to check out your job when I see it posted among hundreds, perhaps thousands of others?

Another important variable in each situation is what is being advertised in your area—newspapers, trade journals, and popular radio and television programs in your neck of the woods. For example, in Rochester, New York, the Smart Dog web site has been read about, talked about, advertised, and marketed quite heavily. However, if you're in Kansas you've probably never heard of Smart Dog and probably never will. So, of course, it wouldn't make sense to advertise your job openings on this site. You may find that niche sites in your hometown work better for you than a huge national site. On the other hand, no matter what town or city you are in, America's Job Bank (run by local and federal labor departments) is accessible to search in libraries and state unemployment offices all over the United States—over 1,800 networked offices free to job seekers and employers. You may need to experiment.

Q: Should I post all my job openings?

A: The answer to this question depends on where you decide to post your openings. If you have three thousand job openings and you decide to go with a job posting service charging by the job order, you will need to receive approval from your CEO to post all your job openings. However, if you decide on a free site or a site offering unlimited job postings for a monthly fee, go for it. You might consider who's going to enter in all those job openings and update them as they are filled. If you feel strongly about posting all your job openings, I recommend you inquire about automatic batch processing. Many of the leading job sites offer this service for little or no cost but don't advertise this service, so you might have to ask a sales representative about it. This process enables the system to extract the information from a file and automatically posts it to the job site.

Q: Do I need to link our web site to job postings on another site?

A: I highly recommend you have a hyperlink to your home page or the employment section of your web site. Why? Because your web site should have everything a potential candidate would want to know about your company. I've talked to a candidate waiting for a job offer after a second interview who didn't even know what the company's core business was. Once he found out, he was no longer interested in the position. I wondered why he didn't do his homework prior to the interview. Once he found out the company didn't make the widgets, but only resold the widgets, he was no longer interested. I highly recommend having your web site linked in some manner. It's also important to mention your web address in print advertisements, brochures, on employees' business cards—wherever you can think of, put it. Be creative–I believe the web address is as important as the postal mailing address. It should be on letterheads and all correspondence.

Another important reason to have your site cross-linked is because key contributing factors to a job seeker's interest in your company are benefits, location of offices and other facilities, and mission statements. Knowledge of these is critical for a good hiring fit. Why waste your valuable human resource staff's time in going over this information when they can just refer candidates to the web site? Job seekers can get a real feel for the culture of the company prior to exploring job opportunities. It is a little-known fact that more job seekers change jobs because of improper fit than for any other reason. They sometimes just don't mesh with the organization's culture, management structure, or size. Some people hate working for companies with more than 500 employees and other people can't work in an organization of less than 500. A well-constructed and properly maintained web site should provide potential job seekers with the chance to test the waters before going for a dip. I know I've nearly drowned a couple of times by not paying enough attention to the corporate culture or doing my pre-job offer acceptance homework. The web site has all the work done for us and all we have to do is drop by to visit.

Q: Should our company post its job listings only on its own web site?
A: No, unless you work for Xerox or some other very large company that everyone has heard of. The big firms can get away with posting their job openings only on their web site because they are big enough that the masses will visit. However, if you are in the other 80 percent of companies that very few people have heard of, you need to join up with some of the big sites that have made it their business to attract attention to their web sites. The other option is for you to spend millions of dollars to advertise your web site so masses of people will come to visit—but why spend money you don't have to? A sales representative from Monster.com recently told me this site alone invests 26 million dollars in advertising campaigns. Even giant Microsoft advertises on job boards.

Q: What kind of response can I expect to receive from my job ads?
A: Again, it depends on many variables. If you have a very lucrative job opening in San Diego paying $250,000 a year with stock options, a BMW, and 15 percent salary increases every two months, you will probably generate many more responses than one of my ads for a database administrator (DBA) paying $55,000 a year in Rochester, New York.

When I placed a display ad for a DBA in the local Sunday newspaper at a cost of $524, I received nine resumes, of which only three met my minimum qualifications. I posted the same ad online (for four weeks) to America's Job Bank's free job site. After four weeks, I received a total of thirty-one inquiries and eleven resumes. This is an average response from an online job posting in the IT field. Some sales jobs posted to America's Job Bank have generated far more inquiries and responses. You have to remember your target audience. Most IT professionals are making very good money and being treated like kings and queens because they are in such high demand. Teasers such as salary, title, an exciting job description, location, flexible working hours, and a chance to work for a growing, profitable, well-known company are all items you need to offer to attract high-demand candidates.

Q: Should I post salary information?
A: My answer is almost always yes. If your salary is competitive with the industry or above average I recommend putting a salary range (such as "70K–85K depending upon experience"). This will give you flexibility but allow you to attract more candidates. If your policy is not to post salary ranges, you might consider saying something like "superior compensation and benefits package offered." If, on the other hand, you are in the lower salary ranges and benefits are a key recruiting tool, by all means stress your strengths and not your weaknesses. Many job seekers nowadays are looking for flexibility in work schedules. The possibility for promotion, growth, and diverse responsibilities weighs more than salary for some job seekers. Statistics have shown job postings (print or online) have a higher response rate when a salary is included.

Q: Is job title really that important?
A: You bet it is! Job title is one of the most important and least understood aspects of online job postings. Too often, employers don't think much about a job title and don't realize that a job title could mean a totally different job in another state. You could ask ten different computer analysts what their job description is and get ten different answers. Think about the job you're listing and do a query yourself on the job bank you're posting to. Find out how many other titles are in the database and think of creative

ways to make your job order stand out. Make sure you use critical words to describe the job in your title. If I were looking for a database administrator, I would post the job as "Database Administrator (DBA)—Oracle." This way someone reading my ad would know I want someone with Oracle experience. Also, if the job seeker did a key word search using the "DBA" rather than "Database Administrator," my job posting would pop up because I have it posted both ways. Remember who your audience is and all the key words they are likely to use in their search

Q: Should we hire one person to handle all the online recruiting for the company?
A: This answer also depends on the size of your company and your resources. If you have an underutilized human resource specialist who can devote some time to online recruiting efforts, you are better off than hiring a new person. If you start gradually you won't have to increase your head count or hire additional temporary personnel to do online recruiting.

Q: Should I be searching resumes online?
A: Yes and no. Online resume databases are a great resource for finding candidates; however, they take extensive amounts of time. If you're looking for very specific individuals or need to fill a critical immediate need, perform as many online resume searches as you can. In Chapter 2 you learned many ways of doing this.

Q: Where's the best place to put an advertising banner?
A: Any one of the leading job sites or portals will provide you with enough exposure to keep your phone ringing and your incoming e-mail box hopping. You might want to ask your service provider several questions, such as: Can they provide a hyperlink to your web site? How many other sites are they linked to? (The leaders will have thousands of other links to their site.) How much do they currently spend on advertising their site? And, how many visitors or hits do they receive per month? You may also want to verify what areas of the country they target.

Q: How long should I keep the job posted?
A: Until it is filled—most job sites do not charge for the amount of time, so you should keep it posted as long as necessary. Be prepared to change

the wording, title, or description if the ad is not generating the response it should be. You should also consider trying another job site if you don't think enough candidates are seeing your job.

Q: How much can I expect to pay for one job ad?
A: The prices of online postings vary as much as the weather does from coast to coast. Prices range from free to as high as $450 per posting. Pricing may go up or down later, but as of this writing I wouldn't pay any more than $500 per posting. Shop around and use the cost chart I developed in Chapter 4 for CareerCity (under Tool 2, Cross-Posting Services) as a guide to help distinguish the gold from the gold plated. They all can't be the best and you can ask for proof before you post. Let your results speak for themselves rather than relying on a site's claim of many hits. You may have already noticed, some of the leading sites post the number of resumes and jobs in their database on their home page. I would much rather compare the actual number of job seekers registered on a site than how many hits a site receives.

Q: Do I have to commit to membership or a yearly contract?
A: Most sites offer a substantial discount if you commit to a quarterly or yearly membership. I highly recommend a membership to lessen your fees once you have decided on a site or two that achieve the results you expect.

Q: Do candidates have to pay to see my job ad?
A: As of this writing, I know of no sites that charge the job seeker for searching the job openings. However, new ones are popping up every day and some greedy entrepreneur might think up a clever way to charge job seekers for viewing job openings. Don't confuse job postings with resume distribution services. Job seekers will pay to have their resumes distributed to recruiters and employers via e-mail or fax. Resume distribution services might charge anywhere from $25 to $450 to distribute job seekers' resumes all over the web into job banks, e-mailed directly to recruiters, or to a targeted fax list. Chapter 3 discussed free ways to sign up with resume distribution services and start receiving fresh resumes in

your e-mail immediately. Job seekers will pay to have their resume cross posted to hundreds of resumes banks, but I'd be surprised if you could get a job seeker to cough up any amount of money to have a resume submitted to just one resume bank.

Q: What are the primary occupations one can search online?
A: In the early days of the Internet (1980 to 1995) the majority of online jobs were in the computer field, research, and the military. Currently, just about every occupation you can think of is online. There is even a site called "cool works" that advertises only cool jobs such as ski instructors, extreme sports trainers, and so on. There is a good mix of all types of careers to be found online—healthcare, engineering, sales, executive, information technology, administrative, and legal, just to name a few.

Q: Is there any way I can tell how many people have read my online job ad?
A: This technology is becoming a necessity. As of this writing, America's Job Bank, Webhire, and a few other sites offer automatic tracking of hits, views, and referrals on their site. I'm anticipating that over the next few years all job sites will incorporate this feature in order to compete by providing measurable results. Again, I must caution you, there are scam artists out there and a company can easily spit out a report that looks authentic but is a phony page view report. So let the results speak for themselves.

Q: Can I do a blind box advertisement online?
A: Yes, just as in print media, you can also do a blind box advertisement online. There are a number of ways you can approach it. One way is to send all responses to a post office box. Another way is to set up an e-mail address and fax number for responses to be sent to. Another choice is to hire an outside contractor to handle all the responses. Be sure to let the contractor know ahead of time you will not pay a finder's fee but only a flat fee to handle the responses and forward only the qualified candidates to you. If you are an employer registered with America's Job Bank, you can use its blind box job posting service and resume screening and forwarding services at no charge.

Q: I want to recruit college graduates. Can I post my jobs at my favorite college(s)?
A: Job Trak and Career Connection are just two leading college-affiliated networks that allow you to post jobs and search recent graduates. These sites and others were detailed in Chapter 6.

Q: What's a newsgroup?
A: A newsgroup is a cross between a newswire and a community bulletin board where people with common interests hang out. They can share ideas and participate in discussions or live chat sessions. Thousands of these groups exist and are detailed in Chapter 5, "The Best of the Freebies." Some newsgroups allow recruiters to post their job listings and/or pose questions to readers. These candid discussions provide invaluable feedback not easily obtained anywhere else.

Directory of Web Sites

DIRECTORY OF RECRUITING WEB SITES

Web Site Name	Web Address	Jobs Data-base	Resumes	Corporate Profiles	Rate	Comments
4Work	www.4work.com	Yes	Yes	No	B+	General site—reasonable prices. Excellent web design with information valuable to job seekers.
AboutWork	www.aboutwork.com	No	No	No	N/A	Superior site for job seekers offering career management, articles, and chat rooms. Powered by Monster.com (and formerly OCC).
AccountingNet	www.accountingjobs.com	Yes	Yes	Yes	N	Accounting niche site—teamed up with CareerMosaic's general site.
America's Job Bank	www.ajb.dni.us	Yes	Yes	Yes	A	Free—thousands of jobs and new-resume database—national site with good networks.
Asia-Net	www.asia.net.com	Yes	Yes	No	N	Jobs for individuals speaking both English and Asian languages.
Best Jobs USA	www.bestjobsusa.com	Yes	Yes	Yes	B	Powered by an ad agency—ads posted here are featured in Employment Review publication and USA Today.
CareerBuilder	www.careerbuilder.com	Yes	Yes	Yes	A+	Top recruitment site—huge networking site. collaborating with many other sites. Received a 5-star rating. Job seekers can search multiple job boards with one search at this site.
CareerCity	www.careercity.com	Yes	Yes	Yes	C+	Several thousand job openings posted mainly from news-groups and corporate links. Great for career services and advice for job seekers.
Careerhighway	www.careerhighway.com	Yes	No	Yes	A	Great recruitment site—partnering with radio to get in touch with passive job seekers. Automatic e-mail notification for job seekers.
Career Magazine	www.careermag.com	Yes	Yes	Yes	A	Great place for career advice and articles—free resume database to search.
Career Mart	www.careermart.com	Yes	Yes	Yes	C	Powered by BSA Advertising (ad agency). Offers automatic e-mail announcements to job seekers when jobs are posted online.

Web Site Name	Web Address	Jobs Data-base	Resumes	Corporate Profiles	Rate	Comments
CareerMosaic	www.careermosaic.com	Yes	Yes	Yes	A	This site is ranked number 1 by Internet Business Network's 1999 Electronic Recruiting Index. Contains thousands of jobs and resumes. Resume database is no longer free—must be a paid subscriber.
Careerpath	www.careerpath.com	Yes	Yes	Yes	B+	Powered by the nation's leading newspapers. this site is great for relocating job seekers. They can search this database for jobs in almost every major city. Price can be high if not advertising in print media.
CareerShop	www.careershop.com	Yes	Yes	Yes	N	Excellent content—targeting IT job fairs, resumes on CD, and cross-posting services. Merged with SelectJobs January 2000.
CareerSite	www.careersite.com	Yes	Yes	Yes	B	Some big-name companies advertise here—good electronic matching capabilities.
Careerspan	www.careerspan.com	Yes	Yes	Yes	B–	Site cross posts to other newsgroups. easy administrative upkeep with a fair price tag.
CareerWeb	www.cweb.com	Yes	Yes	Yes	B	Marketing is good. operated and owned by Landmark and affiliated with The Weather Channel. General job listings by location and category.
Classifieds2000	www.classifieds2000.com	Yes	Yes	No	B	Great site—major attraction with free classifieds. Resume Central coming soon—employers will be able to search database.
College Grad Job Hunter	www.collegegrad.com	Yes	No	No	N	Niche site for college students and recent grads.
Computer Jobs Store	www.computerjobs.com	Yes	Yes	Yes	N	Niche site for IT field in a specific area by region. Will most likely see imitators spread similar sites into other geographic areas.
Computerwork	www.computerwork.com	Yes	Yes	Yes	N	Niche site for IT field in a specific area by region.

DIRECTORY OF RECRUITING WEB SITES continued

Web Site Name	Web Address	Jobs Database	Resumes	Corporate Profiles	Rate	Comments
Dice	www.dice.com	Yes	No	Yes	A & N	Targeting high-tech professionals; engineering jobs also featured. Reasonable price.
DORS	www.dod.jobsearch.org	No	Yes	No	B+	Defense outplacement transition. Job postings via free bulletin service. free resume searches.
Drake Beam Morin	www.dbm.com	Yes	Yes	Yes	B+	Excellent source of free resumes, one of the largest outplacement firms—promote their service to help their clients find jobs.
E-Span	www.espan.com	Yes	Yes	Yes	B+	Changed its name to JobOptions recently—see JobOptions.
Engineering Jobs	www.engineeringjobs.com	Yes	Yes	Yes	N	You guessed it—lots of engineering jobs posted and FREE resumes to search!!!!
HR World	www.hrworld.com	Yes	Yes	—	N	Niche site dedicated to human resources.
Headhunter	www.headhunter.net	Yes	Yes	No	A	Free postings and free resumes—rated number 5 by Internet Business Network's 1999 Electronic Recruiting Index.
Healthcareers Online	www.healthcareers.com	Yes	Yes	Yes	B	Premier site at a reasonable cost. Free resume search with registration. Jobs range from physicians and nurses to clerical jobs (medical billing, etc.).
Healthopps	www.healthopps.com	Yes	Yes	Yes	N	Targets health and medical professionals—affiliated with CareerMosaic.
Hotjobs	www.hotjobs.com	Yes	Yes	Yes	B	Superior site. growing fast. Lists most job categories. Leading technology companies such as Sun Microsystems, Inc., are on board.
Internet Career Connection	www.iccweb.com	Yes	Yes	—	B	Recruitment site run by Gonyea and Associates—resume distribution and matching. Great content.
ICE —Softech Corp.	www.rochesteremployment.com	Yes	Yes	Yes	N	Rochester-based high-tech niche site. All job postings are allowed, but also targets IT professionals.

Web Site Name	Web Address	Jobs Database	Resumes	Corporate Profiles	Rate	Comments
IEEE	www.ieeeusa.org	Yes	Yes	No	N	Niche site—Institute of Electrical and Electronic Engineers—U.S.
JobBank USA	www.jobbankusa.com	Yes	Yes	Yes	C	General site. Some major companies have purchased memberships. Competitive pricing.
Job Net	www.jobnet.com	Yes	Yes	Yes	B−	Offers job fairs, online recruiting seminars, resume bank (targeting mainly the Philadelphia, PA, area).
Job Direct	www.jobdirect.com	Yes	Yes	Yes	N	College students mostly—featured on CNN.
JobOptions	www.joboptions.com	Yes	Yes	Yes	B+	Formerly E-Span, one of the first job sites—has thousands of links, lots of resumes and employment ads.
JobTrak	www.jobtrak.org	Yes	Yes	No	N	Excellent niche site if you are looking for recent MBAs or grads from a specific university—affiliated with hundreds of universities. Very good pricing, too.
JobWeb	www.jobweb.org	Yes	Yes	No	N	Similar to JobTrak. National Association of Colleges and Employers (NACE) sponsors this site.
Jobs4HR	www.jobs4hr.com	Yes	Yes		N	Niche site specifically dedicated to HR.
Monster.com	www.monster.com	Yes	Yes	Yes	A	Rated number 2 by Internet Business Network's 1999 Electronic Recruiting Index. Also teamed up with Online Career Center and TMP Worldwide.
Nationjob	www.nationjob.com	Yes	Yes	Yes	A	General site with thousands of job seekers signed up to receive automatic e-mail notification of job matches via their "P.J. Scout." This site also cross posts to AJB, Yahoo, and Headhunter.
Net-Temps	www.net-temps.com	Yes	Yes	No	A	Resumes, job postings, recruiter splits, online temp hires—excellent site dedicated to recruiters.

DIRECTORY OF RECRUITING WEB SITES continued

Web Site Name	Web Address	Jobs Database	Resumes	Corporate Profiles	Rate	Comments
Online Career Center	www.occ.com	Yes	Yes	Yes	A	Ranked number 7 by Internet Business Network's 1999 Electronic Recruiting Index. Owned by TMP Worldwide and partners with Monster.com.
Recruiters Online Network	www.recruitersonline.com	Yes	Yes	Yes	A	Offers a free thirty-day trial membership. Ranked number 9 by Internet Business Network's 1999 Electronic Recruiting Index.
RecruitUSA	www.recruitusa.com	Yes	Yes	Yes	B+	General site doing an excellent job of marketing to drive candidates to review jobs and post resumes.
Society for Human Resource Management	www.shrm.org	Yes	No	No	N	Niche site for human resource professionals—great resource site for HR-related information & seminars.
TownOnline	www.townonline.com	Yes	Yes	Yes	B+	Superior site for New England area targeting primarily job seekers residing in Maine and Massachusetts.
Transition Assistance Online	www.taonline.com					Recognized as a 5-star site on the Internet for transitioning military personnel.
Virtual Job Fair	www.careerexpo.com	Yes	Yes	No	N	Targets high-tech jobs and resumes, online job fairs; is a nice attraction for passive job seekers.
Wall Street Journal	www.careers.wsj.com	Yes	No	Yes	C+	Excellent career articles with a different perspective from most job sites—geared toward financial and professional job seekers.
Yahoo Classifieds	www.yahoo.com	Yes	Yes	No	A	Excellent high-exposure site—free job postings and searching of resumes.

RATING KEY

A = Superior
B = Excellent
C = Very Good
N = Niche

BEST WEB SITES FOR SPECIALTY AND NICHE RECRUITING

Information Technology (IT) Candidates	Web Address
Developers Net Community	www.developers.net
ComputerJobs Store	www.computerjobs.com
C++ Jobs Dot Com	www.cplusplusjobs.com
Classifieds2000	www.classifieds2000.com
Computer Professionals	www.ohw.com
Programming Jobs	www.prgjobs.com
Jobs4IT	www.jobs4it.com
Bridgepath	www.bridgepath.com
Infoworks USA	www.it123.com
Dice	www.dice.com
PassportAccess	www.passportaccess.com
Placeum 2000	www.placeumit.com
Computerwork	www.computerwork.com
Hotjobs	www.hotjobs.com
ZDNet Job Engine	www.jobengine.com

MBAs and Recent Graduates	Web Address
Bridgepath	www.bridgepath.com
Career Central	www.mbacentral.com
MECA-MBA Employment Connection	www.mbanetwork.com/meca
JobTrak	www.jobtrak.com
Top jobs	www.topjobsusa.com
College Grad Job Hunter	www.collegegrad.com
Job Direct	www.jobdirect.com
College Student	www.collegestudent.com
College Central	www.collegecentral.com
Allcampus Internet	www.allcampus.com

BEST WEB SITES FOR SPECIALTY AND NICHE RECRUITING
continued

Finance or Accounting Candidates	Web Address
100 Careers in Wall Street	www.globalvillager.com/villager/WSC.htm
Accounting.com	www.accounting.com
Accounting and Finance Jobs	www.accountingnet.com
American Association of Finance & Accounting	www.aafa.com
American Banker	www.americanbanker.com
FinCareer Global	www.fincareer.com

Healthcare Professionals	Web Address
Monster Health Care (formerly MedSearch America)	www.monster.com
CareerMosaic (formerly Healthopps)	www.careermosaic.com
Healthcare Jobs Store	www.healthcarejobstore.com
Healthcare Recruitment Online	www.healthcareers-online.com
Med Hunters	www.medhunters.com
Physicians Recruit Net	www.physiciannet.com
MD Direct Recruiting	www.mddirect.com
Medical Jobs	www.medjob.com
Pharmajobs	www.pharma.jobs.com
Physicians Employment	www.physemp.com

Engineering Professionals	Web Address
Engineer Web	www.engineerweb.com
Ednmag	www.ednmag.com
Engineering Jobs	www.engineeringjobs.com
Questlink	www.questlink.com
Summit Design	www.summit-design.com
ASME (American Society of Metalurgical Engineers)	www.asme.org
SAE (Society of Automotive Engineers)	www.sae.org

Diversity	Web Address
Asia Net	www.asia-net.com
Association for Women in Computing	www.awc-hq.org
Association for Women in Technology and Industry	www.witi.com
The Black Collegian Online	www.blackcollegian.com
Equal Opportunity Publications, Inc.	www.eop.com
Diversity/Careers Online	www.diversitycareers.com
National Society of Black Engineers	www.nsbe.com
Latino Web	www.latino.org
Hispanic Online	www.hisp.com
MSBET (Microsoft)	www.msbet.com
Minorities Job Bank	www.minorities-jb.com
Saludos Web	www.saludos.com
Womenconnect	www.womenconnect.com

HR Professionals	Web Address
Society for Human Resource Management	www.shrm.org
Jobs4HR	www.jobs4hr.com
HR World	www.hrworld.com

MISCELLANEOUS WEB SITES

Web Site Name	Web Address	Comments	Chapter
Wageweb	www.wageweb.com	Salary calculator	1
Homefair	www2.homefair.com/calc/salcalc.html	Relocation	1
Job Descriptions Now	www.jobdescriptions.com	Job descriptions	1
Job Search Engine	www.jobsearchengine.com	Multiple job search engine	1
Immigration Help Online	www.immigrationhelp.com/visa.htm	Immigration help	1
iSearch	www.isearch.com	Resume storage service	2
Flip Search	www.flipsearch.com	Resume sourcing	2
GeoCities	www.geocities.com	Online community	2
SkillSearch	www.skillsearch.com	Resume research and search	2
Profusion	www.profusion.com	Mega search engine	2
Cyberdialogue	www.cyberdialogue.com	Surveys online usage	3
LinkExchange	www.linkexchange.com	Banner exchange service	3
Interbiznet	www.interbiznet.com	Online newsletter—free	4
Recruiter's Network	www.recruitersnetwork.com	Online newsletter—free	4
Best Recruiter	www.bestrecruit.com	Online newsletter—free	4
Job Hunt Guide	www.job-hunt.org	Online recruiting resources	4
Riley Guide	www.dbm.com/jobguide	Online recruiting resources	4
It-ta	www.it-ta.com	Resume robot	4
Roverbot	www.roverbot.com	Resume robot	4
Personic Resume Agent	www.ezaccess.com	Resume robot	4
InfoGIST.com	www.infogist.com	Resume robot	4
Anaserve	www.anaserve.com	WebSnake software provider	4
Junglee	www.junglee.com	Middleware software	4

Name	Web address	Comments	Chapter
All In One Submit	www.allinonesubmit.com	Jobs cross-posting service	4
GO Jobs	www.gojobs.com	Jobs cross-posting service	4
Internet Job Locator	www.joblocator.com	Recruiting tool	4
Employ America	www.employamerica.com	Interactive online systems provider	4
Hitbox	www.hitbox.com	Online real-time stats	4
Hotbot	www.hotbot.com	Popular search engine	4
Restrac	www.restrac.com	Resume management service provider	4
Resumix	www.resumix.com	Resume database management tools	4
Resumail	www.resumail.com	Resume management service provider	4
Hire Systems	www.hiresystems.com	Resume management service provider	4
Corporate Organizing and Research Services (CORS)	www.cors.com	Resume research and search	4
Symantec.com	www.symantec.com/avcenter/index.html	Antivirus software and information	4
drsolomon.com	www.drsolomon.com	Antivirus software and information	4
Resume Blaster	www.resumeblaster.com	Resume distribution service	5
Resume Xpress	www.resumexpress.com	Resume distribution service	5
Employment Zone	www.employmentzone.com	Resume distribution service	5
Bridgepath	www.bridgepath.com	Customer relationship management service	5
A+ Online Resumes	www.ol-resume.com/category.htm	Free online resumes	5
America's TV Job Network	www.tvjobnet.com	Free resumes in the media	5
Career America	www.careeramerica.com	Free resumes—entry level	5
Engineering Jobs	www.engineeringjobs.com	Free engineering resumes	5

MISCELLANEOUS WEB SITES continued

Name	Web address	Comments	Chapter
Future Access Resume Inquiry	www.futureaccess.com	Biotech, hardware, software, etc. free resumes	5
Resume Net	www.resumenet.com	Free resumes	5
Deja	www.dejanews.com	Mega sort/search for Usenets	5
Recruit USA	www.recruitusa.com	Similar to Deja	5
Real Cities	www.realcities.com	National network of regional portals	7
CareerXRoads	www.careerxroads.com	Online reviews and comparisons for online recruiting	7
Online Staffing Report	www.sireport.com	Online staffing report	7

Glossary

If you are recruiting online, you are bound to come in contact with unfamiliar terminology. Below are definitions of terms you will most likely encounter in cyberspace.

Access: Getting on or logged onto the system—having access to the information on the Internet. Usually requires some sort of registration or signing up for membership.

America Online: One of the major commercial (for a fee) networks providing Internet access.

AOL: Acronym for America Online.

ASCII: American Standard Code for Information Interchange. Also known as text-only—containing no special formatting codes, such as bolding or underlining. Many companies request that job seekers send their resumes in this format so they can be read on any computer. This is one of two types of files—the other is binary.

BBS: Bulletin Board System services are available through modem dial-up or cable connection and enable conferences, live chat forums, etc.

Baud: Measurement of speed at which information is transferred over a computer modem. Computer analysts sometimes refer to BPS or bits per second; these terms are sometimes used interchangeably.

Browser: A program that helps users search and find information in an easy, time-saving manner on the Internet and web. You are using a browser when you perform a search on Netscape Communicator or Microsoft Internet Explorer.

Caps: All uppercase letters.

CD-ROM: A compact disk with read-only memory, for information retrieval only.

Chat: Real-time exchange of messages via computer. Example: you type words that the other person reads and responds to almost simultaneously.

CompuServe: A very popular commercial (for a fee) network providing Internet access.

Cross posting: A process by which a job is posted online in one location and automatically posted to multiple job sites.

Cyberspace: A term representing the electronic zone or Internet where information is exchanged.

Database: A large amount of data stored in an organized format—always searchable and capable of retrieving stored information. Resume databases are an example of widely used databases on the Internet.

Delphi: Another large commercial (for a fee) network providing Internet access.

Electronic interview: A prescreening of candidates over the Internet via e-mail, videoconference, or chat.

Electronic or scanned resume: A special type of resume stored in computers and resume databases.

E-mail address: Electronic computer address such as careersrus@frontiernet.net used for receiving written messages almost instantly.

Facsimile: Commonly known as fax, a system of transmitting and reproducing graphic matter (print or pictures) via signals sent over telephone lines.

FAQS: Frequently asked questions and answers to the most common questions.

File server: A computer data storage system where programs are shared by many users of a computer.

Freenet: Community-based bulletin board systems funded and operated by individuals. May offer Internet access free or at low cost.

FTP: File Transfer Protocol: program that allows you to connect to another computer and share information—you can view or copy files between the two computers.

Hard drive: The memory storage device built into a computer.

Home page: The first page that comes up when you visit a web site that usually has an index and directory.

HTML: Hypertext Markup Language—the language used to create pages on the web.

Hypertext: Technology used on the Internet that allows linking of documents and home pages for rapid retrieval of data so you can jump back and forth by just clicking your mouse on the word.

Interactive: A two-way electronic communication between user and computer that involves a user's orders (for information or merchandise) or responses (as to a questionnaire).

Internet: The interconnection between computer networks around the world.

IP address: Internet address—usually four groups of numbers separated by periods, such as 120.132.254.3.

Job bank: A centralized listing of private and public notices of job postings.

Key word: A word that denotes important criteria required in your job opening, such as Unix, C++, and MBA degree.

Link: Unit in communication system that allows you to jump from place to place for more information—hot links do the same thing as hypertext.

List: Electronic mailing list or discussion group.

Monitor: The screen that displays information to you.

Netiquette: Internet etiquette—norms of proper behavior on the Internet.

Netscape: An Internet browser.

Network news: Usenet discussion groups devoted to a single topic.

Newsgroups: Usenet discussion groups devoted to a single topic.

Niche site: An online recruitment site targeting a specific industry or profession.

Offline: Not currently online—not connected to or served by a computer system.

Online: Up and running, electronically hooked up—connected to a computer system.

Posting: A job order you place in an online job bank or newsgroup.

Prodigy: Another popular commercial (for a fee) network providing access to the Internet.

Resume bank: A searchable database of electronic resumes you can retrieve by entering specific criteria or key words.

Resume distribution service: An online service such as Resume Blaster where job seekers pay a fee to have their resumes distributed electronically via e-mail to recruiters and employers.

ROM: Read-only memory—cannot be changed, only viewed.

Server: A computer in a network that is used to provide services (access to files, shared peripherals, or routing of e-mail) to other computers in the network—program to find requested documents.

Service provider: An organization that provides access to the Internet.

Site: Location on the Internet where you can access information (see URL).

Subscribe: On the Internet this means adding your name to a mailing list, newsletter, or service.

Teleconference: A long-distance meeting using a telephone—usually participants can see and hear each other with the use of videoconference equipment.

User: The person who is directly using or operating the computer.

URL: Universal Resource Locator—the address of a World Wide Web site.

VDT: Video display terminal or monitor.

World Wide Web: The organized system on the Internet that allows easier navigation of the network through the use of graphic interfaces and hypertext links between addresses.

Yahoo: Commercial–based web service that provides a directory of web sites.

Zip: To compress a file.

References

"BizRate.com: AOL Portal Generates Most Referrals." *Nua Internet Surveys*, Apr. 19, 1999.

"Classifieds Still the Way to Hunt." *CyberAtlas*, Mar. 9, 1999.

Crispin, Gerry, and Mark Mehler. *CareerXRoads*. New Jersey: MMC Group, 1998.

Gates, Bill. *Business at the Speed of Thought*. New York: Warner Books, 1999.

Jandt, Fred E., and Mary B. Nemnich. *Using the Internet in Your Job Search*. Indianapolis, IN: JIST Works, 1995.

Jandt, Fred E., and Mary B. Nemnich, *Cyberspace Resume Kit*. Indianapolis, IN: JIST Works, 1998.

Kennedy, Joyce Lain. *Hook Up, Get Hired! The Internet Job Search Revolution*. New York: Wiley, 1995.

Kennedy, Joyce Lain, and Thomas J. Morrow. *Electronic Resume Revolution: Create a Winning Resume for the New World of Job Seeking*. New York: Wiley, 1994.

"More People Online Without PCs." *CyberAtlas*, Apr. 20, 1999.

"Posting Jobs on the Internet: What Price Awareness?" *Hireadigm*, June 1999.

Useem, Jerry. "For Sale Online: You." Part 3. *Fortune.com*, July 5, 1999.

Index